CRUISING SOUTH

What to expect along the ICW

JOAN HEALY

Editor: Jerry Renninger

Bristol Fashion Publications, Inc.
Harrisburg PA

Cruising South – What To Expect Along The ICW – Joan Healy

Published by Bristol Fashion Publications, Inc.

Copyright © 2001 by Joan Healy. All rights reserved.

No part of this book may be reproduced or used in any form or by any means-graphic, electronic, mechanical, including photocopying, recording, taping or information storage and retrieval systems-without written permission of the publisher.

BRISTOL FASHION PUBLICATIONS AND THE AUTHOR HAVE MADE EVERY EFFORT TO INSURE THE ACCURACY OF THE INFORMATION PROVIDED IN THIS BOOK BUT ASSUMES NO LIABILITY WHATSOEVER FOR SAID INFORMATION OR THE CONSEQUENCES OF USING THE INFORMATION PROVIDED IN THIS BOOK.

ISBN: 1-892216-38-8
LCCN: 2001-132528

Contribution acknowledgments

Inside Graphics: Joan Healy
Cover Design: John P. Kaufman

Cruising South – What To Expect Along The ICW – Joan Healy

Cruising South – What To Expect Along The ICW – *Joan Healy*

Introduction

Don't deny it, because I know better. Time and time again you've whispered to yourself, "Someday I'll go cruising." The words just tumble out. Before I owned a boat, I said it almost daily.

At the time I had no knowledge of seamanship and never imagined it could happen, but over the years I acquired both a boat and some fundamental boating education. I continued to dream and envision turning the dream into reality. As the improbable turned into the distinctly possible, I still harbored doubts about the feasibility of such a venture. I asked myself, "Will I enjoy cruising? Can I adapt to living on a boat?" The eventual answer was yes.

Your first cruise is unique. Anticipation builds as you prepare for an unknown. All the sights and events become priceless experiences as you make the journey.

I viewed the water in a whole new way when it became my neighborhood. Water surrounds and supports you. It's your traveling companion as well as your means of transit. Its color changes daily, alternating between pale tints and deep shades of blue. I ran through brilliant blues that sparkled like diamonds, deep dark blues where no reflections looked back, foamy white tops breaking over blue-green, and brackish water that resembled cheap burgundy. Water can be comforting or threatening, forcing you to harness yourself to the boat as it fights you every step of the way.

I began to connect to nature, almost hypnotized when pelicans folded back their wings and dove from 30 feet to catch dinner. Dolphins played catch-me-if-you can and always won.

Life slows down, and you have time to think and reflect. Deadlines and clocks are left behind. There are no schedules to keep or phones to answer. You begin to live by your own rhythms. The only sound you hear is the lapping of waves, the same sound heard by the earliest mariners.

Each day is golden. The view of New York's skyline from a boat surpasses any postcard. Swans swam to the back of our boat for handouts when we anchored near Solomons Island in Maryland. We saw wild grasses, trees and pristine land interspersed between the cities and towns along the Intracoastal Waterway. Our cruises have graced us with a view of America unattainable by those who roar down the Interstate.

If you're one of those rarefied souls who say, "I'd love to go cruising someday, but doubt it could ever happen." I hope this book will convince you otherwise.

If you can dream it, you can do it.

Joan Healy

Cruising South – What To Expect Along The ICW – *Joan Healy*

Table Of Contents

Introduction   Page 7

Chapter One   Page 13
    How Long Did It Take?

Chapter Two   Page 15
    We Made Lists

Chapter Three   Page 21
    A Pleasure Cruise?

Chapter Four   Page 23
    The Erie Canal

Chapter Five   Page 31
    The Hudson River & Three Days on the Ocean

Chapter Six   Page 51
    Cape May, Delaware Bay, The C&D Canal & The Chesapeake Bay

Chapter Seven   Page 69
    Follow the Magenta Line

Chapter Eight   Page 89
    South Carolina and Georgia

Cruising South – What To Expect Along The ICW – Joan Healy

Chapter Nine   Page 101
    Welcome to Florida

Chapter Ten   Page 115
    Getting Ready to Go Home

Appendix One   Page 119
    Suppliers & Manufacturers

Appendix Two   Page 125
    Tools & Supplies

Appendix Three   Page 135
    Glossary

Cruising South – What To Expect Along The ICW – Joan Healy

Cruising South – What To Expect Along The ICW – Joan Healy

Chapter One
How Long Did It Take?

One of the first questions most people ask when I tell them we took our boat from Buffalo, N.Y., to Florida is, "How long did it take?" The questioner mirrors a culture where time is golden, but we never had a rigid schedule. The cruise was more about the journey, not the destination. We'd decided in advance that if we liked an area, we'd stay as long as we pleased. Thus, the answer was, "As long as we wanted."

I tend to think in terms of how long it took to arrive at the point we considered a trip like this. If someone had asked me when we first started, I would have to say many years ago when I bought a canoe for my husband, Paul. That was the first vessel we owned and we enjoyed it immensely. We were introduced to a feeling of calm and silence that can be perceived only on the water. An idea was instilled in our minds, even though we didn't realize it at the time. After owning a canoe, we thought a sailboat was our destiny as we longed for something bigger to enable us to explore larger bodies of water.

Nonetheless, we were neophytes. We smiled and tried to look knowledgeable as the salesmen told us this boat had a furling system, despite the fact we didn't have a clue what that was. A boom vang sounded downright dangerous to me. Our false show of knowledge didn't fool anyone; the best piece of advice we received was to take a sailing class.

When we couldn't be on the water, we continued to take classes. In addition to basic boating and rules of the road, we learned piloting and navigation. We were learning continually and even beginning to feel we knew what we were doing.

    Many people say if you can sail on Lake Erie, with its short choppy waves, you can sail anywhere. I don't know how true that is, but Lake Erie can kick up some serious storms with little or no warning because it's the shallowest of the Great Lakes. We weathered our share, and our confidence in ourselves and our boat grew. Not only did we become better sailors, we did what all sailors eventually do: we bought a bigger boat, a Niagara 31.

    One day as our time on the water would soon end for the season, Paul said, "Let's keep the boat in next year and go to Florida." I was flabbergasted but as I thought about it, I realized we could. It was decided, and the serious planning began.

Chapter Two
We Made Lists

We wrote down everything and sought out other boaters who had actually done this, looking for encouragement along with advice. We talked to everyone who had made the trip and read books and articles by cruisers. Take advice from everybody and then sort and sift to see what fits you. It's almost impossible to have all the comforts of home. You have to decide what you can live without. Take your time.

Paul's Lists

Paul wanted to make sure the boat was outfitted properly. He tried to anticipate anything that could possibly go wrong and determine what spare parts we needed to carry as repairs during the trip would cut into our budget.

The following list was prepared to ready the boat for departure:

Items with serial or registration number: This file included all the information on each piece of equipment, manufacturer's name and phone number, parts numbers, trouble shooting tips, etc.

Navigation Tools: mechanical pencils, dividers, drawing compass, course plotter, triangles, protractors, erasers. ICW guides from New Jersey to Florida.

Safety Equipment: Distress flag, man-overboard pole with quick release, life jackets, two horseshoe rings, flares and flare gun, whistle, abandon-boat bag for dinghy to include handheld compass, mirror for signaling, small first aid kit, horn, flashlight. (In the event we had to use this, we planned on taking our handheld GPS and VHF radio), fire extinguisher in cockpit area as well as opposite our CNG stove in galley and one forward in the head, binoculars, horn with extra canisters, high quality knife, new storm jib, second bilge pump (1,000 gph) with switch, spare floating winch handle, 50,000 candle power DC spotlight

Maintenance
- Completely wax the hull and topside.
- Fair the keel.
- Paint bottom with good quality paint for salt water (our boat was a freshwater boat until this trip).
- Install two extra pulleys and halyards at masthead.
- Install radar reflector on port spreader.
- Install new zincs.
- Install new rudder bushing.
- Make three mast crutches (used to stow the mast during the trip down the Erie Canal).
- Cans for spare fuel.
- Cans for spare water.
- Change all light bulbs on mast.
- Install new wind, depth, and speed gauges.

Comfort and Convenience
- Handheld VHF to use in cockpit.
- GPS programmed with East Coast light list.
- 10 lb. propane tank and line that could be connected to grill with a bracket to mount on stern pulpit.

Spare Parts
- Engine oil, transmission fluid and funnel.
- Plastic boxes with compartments for screws, nuts and bolts, diesel fuel filters, zincs for heat exchanger, electrical connectors of all sizes, tinned marine wire in various sizes, garden hose repair kits, spare bulbs for all lights on boat, all manner of tape.
- Engine V-belts

- Diesel injectors.
- Impeller repair kit.
- Cleaning supplies.
- Tool boxes. If you don't know what they should contain, a helpful list is in Appendix Two and can be customized to your needs.

My Lists

I was in the habit of making all meals on board, but prior to this cruise, our sailing had been limited to trips of three or four days. At the end of each day we were in a marina. Therefore, I never had to worry about conserving power because I could plug into shore power to recharge our batteries. I was able to use all the gas I needed to cook and bake. If I ran out, it was just a simple matter of changing tanks. Refrigeration was never a problem. Our refrigerator has plenty of space to hold all we needed for a weekend cruise. If I did run short of anything, we would soon be at dock and able to restock. Fresh water was always available at our slip. There was no need to plan meals for weeks in advance.

All this changes when you cruise for an extended period. Our plan was to anchor out as much as possible. Consequently, I had to learn to prepare three meals a day when we might be spending three or four days without getting off the boat. My plans had to include ways to conserve gas, water and electricity. In addition, I needed to have all the supplies on board in case we couldn't get to a store from the anchorage.

I made lists of meals prepared with items that don't require refrigeration and lists of foods with a long shelf life. Many of our favorite recipes worked, so I made a sample menu for 10 days, keeping in mind the size of the refrigerator. Using the menus, I prepared the shopping list to include all the ingredients needed.

Be sure to take a sufficient supply of any items you use regularly that aren't readily available in small stores. I had my favorite cookbooks on board, and as the trip progressed I

Cruising South – What To Expect Along The ICW – Joan Healy

found many new recipes that fit whatever ingredients I had on board at the time. Simultaneously, I learned to use what I had available to make new recipe combinations.

Though we were always able to reach a store within 10 days, it was reassuring to know enough food was stocked for a longer period.

My list for the galley included cloth napkins and place mats, along with pots, pans and good wine glasses. Using cloth napkins cuts down on garbage and also meals seem nicer. In my opinion, wine was made to be drunk in wine glasses. Glasses can be wrapped in old socks to prevent breakage. Napkins and place mats can be used over and over. When they need washed, they can be hung on the life line to dry. When you stock your galley, just think of your kitchen at home.

While you are still dreaming about the wonderful adventures that await, make a list of meals you can prepare in five minutes for the nights you are exhausted. Also think of quick breakfasts so you can leave an anchorage early and get in a good day's sail.

You'll be amazed to discover all the storage on your boat when you really start to look. You also become very ingenious about storing items as the trip progresses. But keep a list of where you put things. It's very easy to forget, especially items that aren't used often. A backpack or granny cart is an absolute must for grocery shopping. It's either that, or you'll increase the length of yours arms carrying supplies back to the boat.

As you plan what clothes to take, think less instead of more. We took too much. You definitely need a rain jacket and pants and a loose-fitting windbreaker that will accommodate a sweater. We experienced some very cool nights and mornings and were glad to have mittens, warm hats and heavy clothing. Shorts, T-shirts and bathing suits became our everyday outfits once the weather stayed warm. Most restaurants near marinas accept casual attire. It's necessary to determine what you'll be doing on the cruise and plan your wardrobe accordingly. Many marinas have laundry facilities. When you are anchored near towns that have dinghy docks, you can also find commercial Laundromats. Quarters for washers and dryers come in handy and can be stored in plastic film containers.

If you plan on sending post cards, bring an address book and a supply of stamps. Take phone numbers you may need, especially doctors' phone numbers.

Be sure to include books when you stock the boat. This trip offers an ideal opportunity to read the classic you've never had time for. We found there's no better place to read than in a quiet anchorage in the evening. We also spent many evenings playing chess, Othello and Mastermind. I had a list of items I now consider my good-intention list that wound up being just that - good intentions. I took paints and drawing pads that were used sparingly and lots of blank notebooks to fill that didn't get filled. I did keep a daily log, but that was the extent of my writing except for postcards and letters. There's so much to see on your first cruise that it's hard to do other things.

The area you'll clean is much smaller than you have at home, and you'll probably use many of the same items. I had read that Joy was good if you had to do dishes in salt water, so I brought Joy. I never had to wash dishes in salt water. I brought a large container of laundry detergent, and when I went to the laundry, I'd fill a small plastic jar to carry with me. All our sundries - soap, shampoo, toothpaste, deodorant, etc., I bought before the trip. A six-month supply is easy to stow.

Don't leave the dock without sun screen and hats. We wore hats continuously. The sun reflects off the water so you'll need good sun glasses. At the end of the day as you head into a marina or anchorage, going west and directly into the sun, makes finding buoys very difficult without good sunglasses.

Clothespins, the spring kind, come in handy for all sorts of uses.

You'll need a good first aid kit that should include aspirin, adhesive bandages, adhesive tape and gauze pads, sterile pads, alcohol, cold pack, A & D ointment, scissors, tweezers, gauze bandages, motion sickness wristbands or tablets, eyewash solution, eye patches, butterfly closures, elastic bandages, sting relief wipes. You also must take a supply of any prescription medication you need along with the prescription. Take your eyeglass prescription in case your glasses break. A good first-aid book is a must, but read it before you need it. I would also suggest taking a good first-aid course that includes basic or advanced first-aid and CPR.

Chapter Three
A Pleasure Cruise?

Before you start compiling the seemingly endless lists, you should determine exactly what kind of a cruise you want. This may strike you as ridiculous, but I assure you it's important to decide beforehand. To some people's amazement, not everyone agrees on what cruising means. The cruise you decide on will determine what you need to provision the boat. If you aren't cruising by yourself, whoever will be with you should help plan the trip to ensure it's a truly pleasurable cruise. Where are we heading? What route will we take? Will we have predetermined destinations? Do we have to be there by a specific date? Will we stay at marinas or anchor out? Will we use the galley for all meals, go to restaurants all the time or a combination of both? Should we wait until we can afford a bigger, more comfortable boat? What will be our set budget for the trip?

Plans can always be changed, but I believe it's extremely important that everyone has some idea of what the trip will entail before departure. You'll encounter lots of surprises, and you don't need to add to the list by having captain and crew not thinking along the same lines. I can only tell you what we did, and it isn't a one-size-fits-all.

We had two major restrictions in our planning. We were limited to six months because we had to return to work. Therefore, we would have to have the boat trucked back. We also were on a limited budget.

The size restrictions of our boat, determined that to

have enough storage we would have to sacrifice the V-berth. For our entire cruise the main cabin doubled as our bedroom. We set up our bed every night and took it down in the morning which took only a few moments. It was a minor inconvenience, but the inflatable mattress was extremely comfortable and provided a queen-size bed, much larger than our V- berth.

The next question: where are we going? For us that was easy. We wanted to spend the winter in warmer climates, as far as the Bahamas. Since we sail on Lake Erie, we had to decide how to reach the Atlantic.

Two ways to stay within a limited budget are to anchor out and cook meals on board. We both agreed that we would do as much anchoring as possible, even though we had not done much overnight anchoring before this trip. I enjoy cooking, so we planned to have most of our meals on the boat. Occasionally we did eat at a restaurant. Because it was only occasionally, we could choose a very nice one and still stay within our budget.

Our dream was to see as much as possible, so we decided before we left that if we liked an area, we'd stay as long as we wanted. We were in no rush.

Take time to think about the trip and what you expect from it, always with the thought that any and all plans can be changed. The whole trip is a learning experience. It's very likely that some of your opinions and expectations will change as the cruise progresses. You may go farther than originally planned or, like us, not go as far as planned. It's the trip itself that is the enjoyment.

Chapter Four
The Erie Canal

The ambivalent feelings I had on our day of departure are etched in my memory. Along with the expectation of a wonderful adventure, there still lurked uneasiness and questioning if we really knew enough. It wasn't until we were cruising for a while and talked to boaters that we realized many first-time cruisers shared this feeling. Many began their trip with the idea, "What we don't know, we'll learn as we go."

We started out with similar thoughts but also had a contingency plan. If it turned out to be more than we could handle or didn't enjoy living aboard, we'd fly home and have the boat trucked back. The only way to find out was to start living aboard. That first day, our anticipation and doubts colliding, kept the adrenaline flowing.

Our son drove us to the marina where our boat waited with her mast resting on crutches. The pre-trip maintenance had all been completed. Each item had been checked off the lists. The supplies and extra parts were on board. Our son helped us carry the final staples to our boat. As he stood in the cockpit and looked down below, I think he was astonished by all the provisions we had crammed inside and probably questioned where we were going to squeeze in. Since this was our first extended cruise, we wanted to make sure we had ample supplies and had stocked the boat accordingly.

We backed out of our slip, waved good-bye and headed out, leaving the skyline of Buffalo with the familiar grain elevators behind us. Looking like a gypsy boat with all the extras that didn't fit below strapped to the outside, we started for the Erie Canal.

Photo 1

We leave Buffalo behind as we head down the Black Rock Canal.

I started the log, noting the time and date, latitude, longitude and weather conditions. We entered the Black Rock Canal which passes under the Peace Bridge that connects Buffalo, New York and Fort Erie, Ontario. The current under the Peace Bridge, as Lake Erie dumps into the Niagara River, is treacherous. After a short distance on the Black Rock Canal, there is a leveling lock to bring boats back into the Niagara River at a point where the current is manageable. From there it's only a short run to the entrance of the Erie Canal that would take us across New York to the Hudson River and the Atlantic.

Cruising South – What To Expect Along The ICW – Joan Healy

Photo 2

The entrance to the Erie Canal from the Niagara River.

As we left the familiar waters of Lake Erie behind, we relied on the red and green markers to lead the way. We were no longer land-bound. We were cruisers.

Canals have locks, and my job in each one was to make sure the bow of our boat didn't swing toward the lock walls. Our mast, on crutches, extended about four feet forward of the bow. I had to sit on the bow holding the line from the lock in one hand and a boat hook in the other to make sure we stayed a safe distance from the wall. The lockmasters check canal passes and ask each captain how far he plans to travel that day. They then notify the lockmasters ahead.

Cruising South – What To Expect Along The ICW – Joan Healy

Photo 3

Each lock has sign showing elevation and distance to next one.

Photo 4

I hold the line and wait for water to raise our boat.

When it was built in 1825, the Erie Barge Canal was the most important waterway in the United States. It provided a route for commerce between the Great Lakes regions of the country and ports on the Atlantic Ocean. At present, most of the traffic on the canal consists of pleasure boats. We did see one tug pushing a barge and learned that commercial traffic still has priority. We heard the tug captain radio the lock as he approached, giving the lockmaster a time of arrival. The lockmaster delayed all pleasure boats to give the tug right of way.

Photo 5

A tug pushes a barge on the canal.

Photo 6

Guard gates: you can see green day marks on the right, indicating you are going to a larger body of water.

Photo 7

A New York State tug boat.

The canal can be a cruise in itself and abounds with history. Many cities that border the canal are in the process of improving their facilities to make them more friendly to pleasure boaters. As we crossed the state, the surroundings changed daily. We were given a glimpse of rural New York, as we passed freshly plowed fields and cattle that had come down to the water for a drink.

Photo 8

Cattle come down to canal to drink.

We met a lot of first time cruisers along the Canal. Some were moving south permanently and had all possessions on their boat. Others, like us, were going for the winter and planned to return in six or ten months. Everyone we spoke to was excited and filled with anticipation about the journey they were starting.

Photo 9

Meantime *shows our hailing port.*

On our last day on the canal the morning began with dense fog, and we decided to wait until it lifted before venturing out. As we sat at anchor, a boat approached from the east and the captain advised us there was no fog two locks to the east. We started out, and as predicted, the fog soon dissipated. After that we passed through an area where the water was absolutely calm. As our boat glided through the water, ellipses formed in the water and spread out behind us. The weather that day ran the whole gamut. Following the fog we experienced sun, clouds, drizzle, encore of sun, strong winds, (cold front coming) heavy downpour and ended with a mix of sun and clouds. It was quite a panorama for our last day on the canal.

Late in the afternoon we reached the Five Steps, the last set of locks that would bring our boat down 150 feet to the Hudson River. After we passed through those last five locks, we had traveled 324 miles and dropped 570' from Lake Erie to the Hudson River, since our trip began. We had spent six days and five nights on the canal, exactly the amount of time we estimated it would take us to cross New York State. We were beginning to feel like seasoned cruisers.

Chapter Five
The Hudson River &
Three Days on the Ocean

When we arrived at Troy, we had to decide where to have our mast stepped. I also had told our children we would call them when we reached Troy. Some lived nearby and wanted to visit us. I found that being on the boat caused me to lose track of days. When I called our one son, I got his answering machine and didn't know what day of the week it was, but did know the date. I left a message on his machine that said as much and later when we talked to him, he said, "That must be quite a trip if you don't even know what day of the week is."

The marina in Troy had laundry facilities, and since we had been traveling for six days, I decided to wash clothes the following morning. As I watched the beautiful morning slip away while waiting for the washer and dryer to end, I realized I shouldn't waste good daylight hours doing this. When we were ready to leave, the sun had disappeared and rain, accompanied by fog, soon began. For the rest of the trip I was better at planning when to do laundry.

Photo 10

Lift bridge Troy, N.Y, one of the most impressive lift bridges on the waterway.

We left Troy, headed south toward Catskill Creek to get our mast stepped and received our first real rock from a tug. When they're not towing or pushing a boat, tugs move prodigious amounts of water as they speed along. After a few wakes like that, I learned to brace my feet if I was at the wheel when a tug was coming toward us and steer into the wake for a more comfortable ride. The rain and fog continued for most of our trip to Catskill Creek. I had to use binoculars all day to find buoys and because of the low visibility, in most instances, I could make out only shapes until we were very close to them. It's imperative on a trip like this that boaters be familiar with aids to navigation, how they are pictured on charts and what they look like on the water. They're the guides that we followed on our whole trip. All the way down the Hudson we looked for green cans on our right as we continued toward the Atlantic.

Cruising South – What To Expect Along The ICW – Joan Healy

Photo 11

Traveling down the Hudson, green marks are on your right.

Photo 12

Green daymark directs boaters to the starboard side of the Hudson.

When we found the entrance to Catskill Creek and started in, we were returning from a larger body of water and knew to keep red markers on our right. We found Hop'Nose, the marina recommended to have our mast stepped. Hop'Nose doesn't take reservations for mast stepping. It's first-come/first-served, so we had to wait a day as there were a number of sailboats ahead of us.

Photo 13

Boats wait at Hop O' Nose Marina.

Before our trip we had no idea so many boats travel this route each year bound for Florida and ports south. The marina staff told us there was a large plaza with a grocery store about one mile away. Since we had a day to spend at Catskill Creek, we decided to do some shopping while we waited. We always took advantage of large grocery stores whenever available.

One immeasurably helpful piece of advice we received when planning our trip was to bring back packs. We found that most of the time we had to walk a mile or more to a store and were surprised to find how much additional weight we could carry on our backs, as compared to carrying it in our arms.

As soon as the mast was back up, we felt like sailors again. We left Catskill Creek and headed into the Hudson River. Although we did follow a chart book in the canal, our real charting began in the Hudson. Before we started our trip, we had talked to a boater who had spent considerable time on the Hudson. He told us how important it was to stay between the buoys because the deepest part of the river was not, necessarily, in the center.

Photo 14

Buoy keeps boats away from rocks.

Since we depended on charts daily, keeping them in good shape was a concern. Space was limited, and a great many charts were needed for a trip such as this. We kept them rolled in a large tube under our galley table to keep them from getting damaged. The chart books and all our charting materials were kept in the chart table. I'd spread out the charts and materials out on our table as needed to study the course. I made it a practice to look ahead on the charts to determine what to expect. When I wasn't busy doing chart work, I enjoyed the wonderful view along the Hudson River.

Photo 15

Lighthouse at Kingston entrance to Roundout Creek.

Photo 16

Middle Hudson Light.

Cruising South – What To Expect Along The ICW – Joan Healy

After leaving Catskill Creek, we headed to Kingston, where the town dock is right in the city. The dock was similar to a parking lot. Since we weren't planning to stay overnight, we paid by the hour, and spent a few hours walking through the town sightseeing. After leaving the town dock we anchored in Roundout Creek.

Photo 17

Downtown dock at Kingston.

Photo 18

Dinghy ride back to anchorage in Roundout Creek.

The next day on our way to West Point, the Hudson took us to Polopels Island at the northern entrance to the Highlands. As we approached we saw what appeared to be a castle, which is Bannerman's Island Arsenal. The structure, in the style of old baronial Scottish architecture with battlements and towers, was built in the early 1900's by an arms dealer from New York City.

Photo 19

Bannerman's Arsenal stands majestic near the entrance to the Highlands.

West Point was our next planned stop. Here we learned about anchoring in a strong current. The fact that it was a popular anchorage with many boats already there didn't make the lesson easier. After several unsuccessful attempts, we realized the bottom dropped abruptly from 12' to 45'.

As we proceeded down the Hudson, the water got saltier, ships got larger and the ports of call on the ships identified countries far away.

Photo 20

A tug with a large push in the Hudson.

Photo 21

The tug attaches to the stern of the barge using heavy cables.

Photo 22

This tug is pulling the barge.

We spent a night at Tarrytown. For boaters who wish to visit New York City, this location is ideal. Directly across the street from the marina you can catch a train to Grand Central Station. Some of our children visited us while at Tarrytown. They offered to take our mast crutches and store them for future trips, and helped put our dinghy onboard. We had trailed the dinghy through the canal and this far in the Hudson, but for our venture into the Atlantic, we wanted the dinghy on board. We didn't want to worry about it breaking free if we encountered rough seas.

After passing under the Tappen Zee Bridge, we confronted a portion of the Hudson that presented an obstacle course. We had to constantly watch the water ahead to find a clear passage through large pieces of floating debris. As Paul watched one side and I the other, we had to steer a zigzag course to evade logs and lumber.

As we approached Manhattan, buildings crowded the sides of the river. Huge apartment buildings looked as if they could house our hometown and skyscrapers filled our field of vision.

Photo 23

Boats line the docks with New York City in the background.

Water taxis shared the river with us along with tugboats, freighters, ferries, large cruisers and other sailboats.

Many large cruise ships lined the docks. Overhead, helicopters rushed important passengers to destinations we could only imagine.

Photo 24

A New York City ferry.

    We had planned to anchor behind Liberty State Park, but small craft warnings were posted and severe thunder storms expected. All boats in the area were being advised to seek shelter. We decided a marina would be better than anchoring for the night, so we found a marina on the New Jersey shore. As the lights came on across the river in New York City, the whole town seemed to glisten. The marina was almost directly opposite the World Trade Center, so we had a postcard view of the Big Apple.
    Early in the morning as we left the marina and sailed past the Statue of Liberty and Ellis Island, I wondered what thoughts filled the minds of all those who came to this country. Their adventure dwarfed ours but, like us they must have questioned where it would lead them.

Cruising South – What To Expect Along The ICW – Joan Healy

Photo 25

Statue of Liberty.

We had heard stories about congestion and confusion as you cross New York harbor. We had to be vigilant, especially near the Verranzano Narrows Bridge, because ships were headed in every direction. We had to watch not only ahead and both sides, but also astern for overtaking vessels. We saw container ships waiting to be called into port, tugs with barges, tugs that were being refueled, the Staten Island Ferry, and water taxis.

New York harbor has more than one channel leading to the Atlantic. As the navigator, it was my job to determine which one to follow and then find the buoys that designated it. There are also shoal areas that we had to avoid. From the harbor we sailed around Sandy Hook and into the Atlantic.

Photo 26

Container ship beneath Verrazano Narrows Bridge.

Cruising South – What To Expect Along The ICW – Joan Healy

Photo 27

A tug refuels on the water.

Photo 28

Staten Island Ferry crosses the river.

Our first day of ocean sailing was all we could have asked for, and more. The sun was shining and wind was perfect, with following waves that helped push us along. We even beat our hull speed, a sailor's dream come true. Since conditions seemed perfect, we sailed right past the first inlet at Manasquan and chose to keep going.

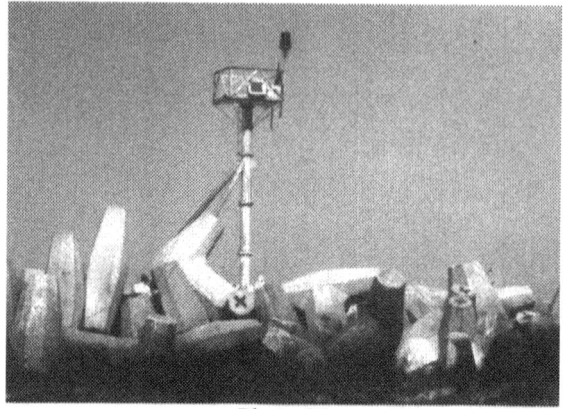

Photo 29

The rocks at Manasquan Inlet are far from inviting.

    Late in the afternoon we decided to stop for the day at Barnegat Inlet, not knowing at the time that we were about to face our first repair. As we lowered the sails and started the engine, we noticed it sounded strange. A look over the stern confirmed the engine was not pumping water, so now we were approaching our first inlet trying not to use our motor. Paul let out the jib and we tried to sail in, but this proved futile. So he started the engine and I watched the temperature. As soon as it started to heat up, he turned off the engine and we would sail as best we could. We hobbled along in this manner, wondering if we could do this repair ourselves.

Photo 30

The red lighted daymark leads boats into Barnegat Inlet.

Cruising South – What To Expect Along The ICW – Joan Healy

Photo 31

A Corps of Engineers boat heading out of Barnegat Inlet.

The entrance is well marked and I had reviewed the chart, but because we were more concerned with reaching a place to anchor and fix our engine, we headed straight toward a boat at anchor, ignoring the buoys. Never do that. Buoys are in place for a reason, and we soon learned that the hard way. As we headed toward the anchored boat, I noticed birds "standing on water." In only a moment, we were aground. A Boat/U.S. tow boat approached to see if we needed help. Paul said he was going to take an anchor out in our dinghy and try to kedge off, but first wanted to find out what was wrong with the engine. The tow boat operator informed us we didn't have time as the tide was going out and we would soon be on our side.

That was all the convincing we needed. He towed us to the anchorage. We had towing insurance, but the towboat operator suggested we increase it since we were headed to Florida, and we took his advice. On this trip we noticed an abundance of tow boats. The farther south we went, the more tow boats we saw, especially near inlets. We met boaters later in our cruise who had been towed long distances and were extremely happy they had unlimited towing insurance. One of the best, widely located and inexpensive is SeaTow.

The next day was spent replacing the impeller. A few

years earlier we had an impeller replaced at our marina and Paul watched so he would know how to replace one. This knowledge came in handy now. The repair took a full day because the impeller was in an area that was hard to reach. Our new batteries had to be removed along with the battery box installed in the starboard lazarette. The cockpit was soon overflowing with tools, tool boxes, batteries and battery boxes. Paul did all the repair, but I assisted. There were areas where his hands wouldn't fit, so I had to squeeze my hands in there. I'm convinced that whoever designs boats and the placement of engines must imagine all boat mechanics to be of very small build.

After spending a portion of the day upside down in the lazarette on one side of the engine while Paul was on the other, the old impeller was out and a new one in. Paul started the engine, but still no water was coming out. Our friend from the tow boat came back to see how we were making out and told us that the fins on the impeller had to face in the proper direction. Once again the impeller was removed, fins checked and the impeller replaced, but still no water pumped out. The tow boat operator had given us the phone number of a diesel mechanic. The mechanic told us, if rubber pieces from the old impeller were in the heat exchanger, that would also stop the water flow. When the heat exchanger was removed, we found small pieces of impeller inside. After cleaning out the heat exchanger and adding new anti freeze, the water pump worked fine.

Little things can make you extremely happy. We also experienced a nice feeling of accomplishment, knowing we could perform our own repairs. Once more we believed we knew what we were doing and were anxious to head south the next day.

Photo 32

Paul is prepared for anything.

Next morning as we left Barnegat Inlet, doubts resurfaced as we faced an ocean that seemed not at all related to the one we had just experienced. Although the weather forecast called for northwest wind and we were sailing south, we were sailing dead into the wind and waves were crashing over our bow.

As I recall that day, I think the seas were more uncomfortable than unsafe, but we were brand-new at ocean sailing and didn't know what to expect. We both wore harnesses strapped to the boat. We also noticed there were very few other boats insight. One boat that had left before us turned around and went back. We wondered if that captain was smarter than we were. After about four hours the New Jersey shoreline hardly changed. We motor sailed and did a lot of tacking, finally reaching Atlantic City. I was very relieved when we pulled into the Marina at Atlantic City and so thankful others didn't say, "Oh, that's typical ocean sailing."

Cruising South – What To Expect Along The ICW – Joan Healy

Photo 33

The inlet at Atlantic City with the casinos in background.

The forecast for the following day sounded like the seas were really going to be violent so we decided to stay a second day at Atlantic City. On the third day the forecast looked good, so we decided to depart for Cape May and Delaware Bay.

At Atlantic City we made our first serious mistake. We had just started filling our water tanks when we realized we were putting water into the diesel tank. This had the potential to be a very costly error. Instead, it taught us how helpful other cruisers can be. Our neighbors to starboard heard about our problem and offered to help with their filter and siphon. They came aboard, siphoned and filtered and filtered some more as we sat and watched. Soon our fuel tank held only diesel. We thanked them profusely and wanted to buy them lunch. Their reply was that they had helped us today, and someone else will help them if they needed it down the line.

Most cruisers consider this an unwritten rule and are always available to offer encouragement, advice and assistance.

We wanted to leave Atlantic City on that particular day because the weather forecast for the next day sounded ideal to cross Delaware Bay. We started out and encountered a second day of going into wind and waves as we headed to Cape May, even though the forecast again had called for northwest winds.

Cruising South – What To Expect Along The ICW – Joan Healy

We were beginning to have some doubts about the weather forecasts, but we did feel more confident on the ocean. We knew we could handle it.

Cruising South – What To Expect Along The ICW – *Joan Healy*

Cruising South – What To Expect Along The ICW – Joan Healy

Chapter Six
Cape May, Delaware Bay, The C&D Canal & The Chesapeake Bay

After our third day on the ocean, we had sailed down the coast of New Jersey and arrived at Cape May where we anchored in front of the U.S. Coast Guard station. At 0740 a large Coast Guard boat, the stern deck crowded with crew, passed us, while on shore a Coast Guard unit was executing a morning drill. All the way down the coast I was impressed by the very visible presence of the Coast Guard.

The morning looked promising. The forecast for a good day was going to be accurate. We had been told Delaware Bay could produce nasty sailing conditions, and we wanted to cross with good weather. We entered the Cape May Canal, which took us into Delaware Bay. Once in the bay we were able to sail for a while, but as the day progressed, the wind lessened and after a few hours there was none. It became a struggle for the helmsman to keep on course.

Delaware Bay lived up to its reputation. We were reminded of Lake Erie as we crossed another shallow lake that could produce rough conditions with little or no wind. We started the engine to finish our trip, and in a short while we were also battling current that was heading out toward the Atlantic. Our speed over the ground diminished. We were also losing daylight and determined we needed to find an anchorage for the evening.

We started searching for the Cohansey River mentioned in the anchorage guide. We followed the directions to the specified buoy given in the guide but were unable to locate the mark. The whole bank of the bay looked like a field of tall grasses with no sign of an entrance. We spotted a mast in the grasses and knew there was a sailboat at anchor in there. We used binoculars but were unable to pick out an opening or see the buoy. As luck would have it, the captain of another sailboat ahead of us found the entrance and as he headed in, we followed, constantly checking our depth. We made our way carefully and eventually found a good spot to anchor.

The next morning we awoke to dense fog and wondered if we should wait until it lifted. As the other sailboats started to leave the anchorage, we decided to follow them out of the river and into Delaware Bay. The current in the bay was much friendlier this morning.

Photo 34

Red daymark in the fog of the Delaware Bay.

Photo 35

A light house in the middle of the Delaware Bay.

The Delaware River took us to the C & D Canal, used extensively by commercial traffic. There are times when pleasure boats are restricted. Red and green flashing lights are positioned at either end, Reedy Point and Town Point Wharf, being the two entrances.

Photo 36

Green light signals pleasure boats can enter C & D Canal.

Photo 37

A tug goes in the opposite direction in C & D Canal.

Photo 38

This railroad bridge is raised unless a train is approaching. Boaters should monitor Channel 13 for the status.

At the far end of the canal we arrived at Chesapeake City. Here the buoys reversed, and we were again going towards the ocean with green cans on the right side as we headed out into Chesapeake Bay.

If someone asked me what I remember most about the Chesapeake, I would have to answer, "Crab pots everywhere, and a plethora of sailboats." We saw enormous sailboats, small daysailers, sloops, ketches, cat boats, gaff rigged boats, and schooners. We watched sailboat races and large sailboats that took passengers for hire. The bay brimmed with sailboats.

We sailed to the Sassafras River and decided to stop at a marina to change the engine oil. The mechanics at Georgetown Yacht Basin were very helpful, answering questions and even loaning tools to make the job easier. I borrowed a bike from the marina and did some grocery shopping. With the oil changed, fuel and water tanks full and groceries restocked, we headed back into Chesapeake Bay.

We crossed the bay and entered the Patapsco River, which teemed with the activity of the thriving port of Baltimore. We passed under the Francis Scott Key Bridge and past Fort McHenry to the city of Baltimore. We stayed at the Inner Harbor East Marina, within walking distance of the Inner Harbor and Fells Point. A multitude of shops and restaurants as well as street entertainers and museums made Inner Harbor a favorite place for tourists as well as city residents.

Photo 39

A bridge fender at the bridge on the Patapsco River entering Baltimore's Inner Harbor.

Photo 40

Baltimore's Inner Harbor docks with the city's skyline.

Then we were on to Annapolis in time for the boat show and it looked as if every other sailor was there also.

Photo 41

Entrance to Severn River.

Cruising South – What To Expect Along The ICW – Joan Healy

Photo 42

Annapolis is said to be the largest sailing community on the eastern seaboard.

Several boats were anchored in front of the Naval Academy, so we decided to stay there also. It was a real treat to sit in the cockpit and listen to the Naval Academy marching band practice. But anchoring there proved to be very uncomfortable. It's nice to be rocked to sleep, but the rocking that anchorage provided was a little too much. When morning came, we were both ready to move. Paul took our dinghy to find the entrance to Back Creek. When he returned, we pulled up the anchor to find a spot among the many other boats.

Photo 43

This is a very tight anchorage with little swinging room.

A Coast Guard boat came through to make sure the channel was open. A few boats anchored between the red and green buoys were told to move. The second day of our stay the harbor master came to each boat with a welcome letter and rules about the anchorages at Annapolis.

We stayed five nights, which was the first time we had anchored in one spot more than one day. We had neither a genset nor wind generator and knew that while at anchor the power would drain from our batteries. Refrigeration especially draws a great deal of power. This was no problem when we were moving every day and using our engine an hour or two a day. In order to keep our batteries up while anchoring, Paul would run the engine for an hour or two in the evening until our battery monitor read 13.8 volts. This worked fine for our stay at Annapolis and throughout our cruise.

We took our dinghy to one of the docks so we could walk into town and found that dinghy docks are just like parking lots. They fill up on a weekends especially when the boat show is in town. It drizzled for a few days while we were in Annapolis and the natives all said, "It's raining. It must be boat show week." We put on rain slickers and looked like everyone else. The yellow slickers gave us some protection from the rain, but we still had our share of wet clothes to dry in the small area of a boat. The drizzle and rain we experienced at Annapolis convinced me that the worst part of cruising is the dampness when you can't get clothes to dry. The inside of our boat took on the atmosphere of a laundry with damp clothes hung all over. When the sun is shining, there's no problem. At the end of the week the sky cleared and we decided to leave.

As we sailed Chesapeake Bay, I was constantly reminded of the large number of people who earn their living on the water. On Lake Erie, we'd see a few small boats out for the day and, occasionally a commercial fishing boat out in the middle of the lake. In stark contrast, on the Chesapeake we saw scores of large commercial fishing boats and crab boats daily. They were always ready to leave at the crack of dawn and prepared to spend a full day working on the water.

Cruising South – What To Expect Along The ICW – Joan Healy

Photo 44

The gulls are always ready for free food from the fishing fleets of the Chesapeake.

Conditions on the Chesapeake can change rapidly. It doesn't take a lot of wind to make the bay kick up. One night after anchoring in a river just off the bay, we noted the calm water and went for a swim. A short time later we experienced choppy waves, had to pull up anchor and go farther up the river to gain protection from the weather.

Photo 45

Daymarks show the way to the narrow channels.

Photo 46

One of the "modern" light houses.

We crossed the bay to visit St. Michael's and Oxford, two cities that were recommended because of their history. The task of finding an anchorage for the night was becoming less of a chore. We would check our anchorage guide for a location, look for other boats at anchor and join them. Then we would take our dinghy into the dock and walk through the towns. After being on the boat all day, it always felt good to walk and stretch, and we wanted to see everything, one of our reasons for the trip. Walking is the ideal way to experience new towns. Our walks enabled us to see what was unique in each area, especially the architecture, some houses being hundreds of years old. As we strolled down the streets, we felt we were looking at a page out of history. We wandered in and out of the shops noting the food in that particular region and galleries where crafts were made by local artists.

Photo 47

Point No Point Light keeps boats off the rocks.

Photo 48

Smith Point Light is at the border between Maryland and Virginia.

We sailed south on the Chesapeake to the Patuxent River on our way to Solomons Island. Navy jets treated us to an air show as we entered the river just as they were returning to base at the end of the day.

Photo 49

Preferred-channel marker at Solomons Island.

Photo 50

A Swan at Solomons Island looking for a handout.

    We went up another Back Creek to anchor where swans came up to the boat to be fed. We anchored a few more evenings in some of the many peaceful rivers and streams that lead into the bay. It was a nice experience to wake up to a new sight each morning.

Cruising South – What To Expect Along The ICW – Joan Healy

Photo 51

Wolf Trap Light leads boats to Hampton Roads.

Photo 52

Entrance light at Hampton Roads.

After almost a month, we entered Hampton Roads where the battle of the Merrimack and Monitor was fought during the Civil war. The supremacy of ironclad ships was established during this battle leading to our present day battleships, and we would see them soon.

Cruising South – What To Expect Along The ICW – *Joan Healy*

Photo 53

Paul weighs anchor, with Hampton Welcome Center in background.

At Hampton, Va., there's an anchorage in front of the building that houses their Welcome Center, a sign of southern hospitality. The city provides a dinghy dock, allowing easy access to visit the area. When we stepped off the dock, we were in town.

Photo 54

Cruising South – What To Expect Along The ICW – Joan Healy

Photo 55

Fishing boats at Hampton, Va.

Hampton was another city that had preserved its past. During our visit, we rode a restored carousel and walked past St. John's Church, built in 1610. As we left the next morning, huge ships were silhouetted on the horizon as we again crossed Hampton Roads. We went from remembering historic battles to viewing present day naval power when sailing past Norfolk. Their size and abundance is astonishing.

Photo 56

Photo 57

Photo 58

U.S. Navy ships at Norfolk, Va.

We were no longer in the wide bodies of water of the Chesapeake and Delaware Bay and would soon enter a narrow channel.

Just past Norfolk is Portsmouth, where colossal cranes are ready to handle cargo on the large ships that line the shoreline. Watching these container ships from a distance as we were cruising, they appeared to be carrying building blocks of many colors. Up close I realized each block was the large trailer of a tractor trailer truck. As usual, tugs were busy hurrying to and fro and in between all the other activity, a dredge was working to keep the channel deep and wide. We had just passed mile number one of the Intracoastal Waterway or ICW.

Photo 59

Senator *was one of the huge container ships near Portsmouth.*

Photo 60

Bright-yellow cranes load barges.

Photo 61

The tugs work 24/7.

Photo 62

Container cranes load the ships.

Photo 63

Ubiquitous cranes.

Photo 63a

A laden ship starts out.

Chapter Seven
Follow the Magenta Line

On the chart the ICW appears as a magenta line. As we traveled it we cruised on creeks, rivers, lakes, bays, channels, canals and sounds. Many of these bodies of water, plus the inlets from the Atlantic, have buoys marking them that are not ICW markers. Boaters on the ICW must constantly make certain that the buoys they follow are marked with ICW marks (yellow squares or triangles on the green and red markers). We always took the time necessary to verify which buoys were correct. In addition, we had to pay attention to the numbering sequence. As we passed certain areas, the numbering would start over at one or two, or change to a completely different sequence. There were times when we had to keep red markers on our right side (red, right, return) and at other times this reversed and we had green markers on our right. The marks on each body of water tell boaters if they are going to or returning from, a larger body of water. The charts gave us all this information, and thus before we got to the buoy, we knew what we were looking for.

Photo 64

Green day marker with yellow triangle, signifying it's an Intracoastal navigation aid.

Photo 65

Green light and daymark on ICW.

Some areas of the ICW are wide, where we enjoyed a good sail. In others we were confined to a narrow channel and had to stay in the middle to keep enough water under our boat. We found many areas of "skinny" water along the ICW. This problem occurs most often where the ICW is near an inlet. In these areas the bottom silts, and dredging operations have a

hard time keeping up. There are numerous tow boats in these areas looking for customers, so if the need arises, help is never far away.

A short distance past Portsmouth we passed the Jordan lift bridge and the Gilmerton bascule bridge. These were just a preview of the numerous bridges we would encounter on the ICW.

Photo 66

The Jordan lift bridge.

Photo 67

Gilmerton bascule bridge.

Soon after passing these two bridges, boaters must decide whether to go through the Dismal Swamp or the Virginia Cut. We chose the Cut, hoping to have enough water under the boat. This was not always the case.

On the first day we started counting the miles to Florida. We were still in Virginia, but this part of the state was very rural and heavily wooded with no large towns or cities in view, in stark contrast to all the activity at Norfolk and Portsmouth. Some fishermen wearing camouflage outfits and orange hats passed us, but the waterway was very quiet.

Photo 68

Marker at mile 105 with red daymark and light.

Cruising South – What To Expect Along The ICW – *Joan Healy*

Photo 69

ICW Mile Marker 120 stands alone.

Knowing the distance to our chosen marina, we calculated we should be able to reach it by the end of the day. However, we experienced a long wait at the Great Bridge Lock, the only lock on the ICW. We were still hoping to reach the marina when we finally exited the lock, even though we still had a good distance to travel. As the afternoon wore on, we started losing daylight and it was becoming more difficult to see the buoys and determine if we were in the middle of the channel. To add to our problem, this particular stretch of the waterway had buoys on only one side, with a lengthy distance between them. Even with good light it was difficult to ascertain if we were in the middle of the channel.

One way to help verify that you are in the channel when limited to buoys on only one side is to watch the buoys behind you. If you can see two or three, your wake will tell you if you are in the channel. In most instances this should help to keep you mid-channel, but sometimes even doing this isn't enough and you run into difficulties. As said earlier, it's important to stay in the channel because there are many shallow areas just outside.

We found one as we were admiring a beautiful sunset and ran aground. Paul took a small anchor out in the dinghy to kedge off, but it wouldn't hold in the muddy bottom, so he tried a large, heavy anchor, which held. After much winching, we were free, only to immediately hit ground again. Happily, we were able to back off this time. By now it was too dark to attempt going any farther, so we anchored just outside the channel with a good anchor light. We soon discovered that most sailboats go aground at one time or another. We bumped bottom many times. A captain of a catamaran told us, "Anyone who says they never went aground coming down the ICW is lying." Later in our trip we talked to many boaters who had chosen the Dismal Swamp Canal. They had no problems with depth although a few did bump logs.

Our knowledge of cruising and living aboard was growing every day. I soon learned to interpret the waterway guides. I'm not sure who wrote the descriptions of marinas and services they offer. I know when they list groceries at a marina, their idea of groceries differs, greatly from mine. I tend to think of items such as eggs, milk and bread. Nothing fancy, just a few staples. Conversely, marinas stock snack foods, beer and maybe canned soup or tuna, usually items that have a very long shelf life. We found that if the waterway guide said a grocery store was within walking distance, there would be a much better chance of being able to get supplies we needed. Whenever a large grocery store was available, we stocked the lockers.

On a sunny day we crossed Albemarle Sound and entered the Alligator River.

Cruising South – What To Expect Along The ICW – Joan Healy

Photo 70

Alligator River Swing Bridge.

We were in North Carolina and had our first taste of 80-degree weather on the trip. The chart noted that there are many logs in the Alligator River and cautioned boaters to watch for them. A boater ahead of us called on Channel 16 to warn others of a submerged log that looked like a crab buoy located between marker 31 and 33.

Photo 71

Watch for logs in Alligator River.

Photo 72

Fairfield Swing Bridge at Alligator River and Pungo Canal.

We saw our first dolphin in North Carolina and were greeted by a whole family of them as we entered South River. In North Carolina the ICW follows the path of many rivers, including the Alligator, Pungo, and Neuse.

Photo 73

Bridge warning sign.

Some were wide and seemed more like lakes, which allowed us to sail. Others provided peaceful anchorages for cruisers, as well as environments that welcomed dolphin. We anchored in some of the rivers as we headed toward Beaufort, where we planned to stay a while.

Photo 74

Channel marker as Pungo River and Pamlico River join.

Photo 75

Coast Guard station in Hobucken, N.C.

Photo 76

Fishing boats line the side of the channel in Hobucken.

Photo 77

Coast Guard tug and work barge in N.C.

In Beaufort, we learned a maritime museum was nearby. We walked there and enjoyed a display of thousands of shells all named and cataloged. There were also displays of the history of boat building in area. The museum has no admission fee, but does accept donations. The marina had a courtesy car that we used to get to a grocery store and a hardware store. We stayed at Beaufort an extra day because the weather turned cold and we wanted to plug in our heater for the night.

As usual, we studied the chart before leaving. When we found it confusing, we went to a marine store to get a chart that was easier to read. But even this chart was hard to follow because of the number of markers all in one small area. There are buoys for the inlet and buoys leading ships to Morehead City and Beaufort. Pleasure boats, coming out of Beaufort, have to round Radio Island and go to a turning basin to get back into the ICW, but have to be careful to follow the correct buoy so they don't turn too soon. The morning we left, the area was crowded. We knew what number buoy we had to find and were extremely careful to pass it on the correct side. One of the sailboats that had left before us was on the rocks with a Coast Guard boat rendering assistance. We assumed they had trouble finding the correct buoy and had turned the corner too soon.

Photo 78

Stay clear of the rocks as you round Radio Island when leaving Beaufort heading for the ICW.

We found our way to the turning basin and into the channel. Just past Morehead City we saw, from a distance, what appeared to be many boats anchored in the channel.

These, in fact, were small fishing boats slowly crossing the channel, forcing us to run a zigzag course to avoid them.

Photo 79

Fishing boats in the channel provided an obstacle course.

After leaving Morehead City we entered Bogue Sound, which looks large but the channel is very narrow. Sand bars on both sides were a constant reminder to stay in the channel. We were passing behind the Outer Banks of North Carolina.

Photo 80

Sandbars at Bogue Sound in N.C. skirt the ICW.

Cruising South – What To Expect Along The ICW – Joan Healy

Photo 81

One of the many work vessels.

After traversing the sound we entered a channel that leads to the Marine Corps' Camp Lejeune. Signs along the banks prohibit landing. There are times when this stretch of the waterway is closed because of artillery and small arms firing and landing exercises.

Photo 82

Warning signs at Camp LeJeune.

Later we also heard areas of the ICW in Florida would be closed if a space shuttle was to be launched at Cape Canaveral. These notices were always broadcast days in advance so boaters could plan accordingly. We always monitored Channel 16 when we were traveling.

Photo 83

Onslow Swing Bridge is open to let boats pass.

Cool weather continued the day we left Beaufort, but we still planned to anchor for the night, and that meant no heater. Before going to bed we put on sweatsuits, wool socks and watch caps. When we awoke, the temperature in the cabin was 49 degrees, but the sun was shining and we knew it would soon warm up.

Photo 84

Anchorage at Mile Hammock Bay at sunset.

Cruising South – What To Expect Along The ICW – Joan Healy

Photo 85

A Pepto Bismal pink house on the ICW in N.C. south of Alligator Bay. From this point on the architecture begins to resemble Miami.

Countless bridges span the ICW. They are noted on the charts and in waterway guides. Clearance under each bridge is also noted on your charts. This does vary, however, due to tide fluctuations, which can be significant in some areas. As you approach, you'll see markers that show the exact clearance at that time.

Photo 86

Bridge marker showing overhead clearance.

As for lift bridges, some open on demand, but many have set times. We learned to plan our arrival to coincide with an opening. It's important to find this out before arriving at a bridge at 7:15 a.m. and waiting for over an hour.

Photo 87

Boats circle waiting for Surf City Bridge to open.

Photo 88

Proper time reduces the wait.

One bridge we didn't pass through easily was the Figure Eight Bridge.

As the bridge opened, Paul put the boat into forward. There was no response. He tried reverse. No response. After quickly checking the transmission fluid and determining that was not the problem, we dropped anchor. The bridge operator called to ask if we were going to pass through. We told him we were experiencing problems so he wouldn't hold the bridge open for us. We called BoatU.S. and were towed to the Masonboro Boat Yard. We had to pass the Wrightsville Bridge and learned that restricted bridges open on demand for all commercial traffic, including boats in tow. If you happen to be waiting for a bridge opening when a commercial vessel requests an opening, you also can pass.

Photo 89

Wrightsville Beach Bridge is a favorite spot for fishermen.

We knew that transmission problems were something we were not able to handle ourselves but found a mechanic to make the repair. We were encouraged upon arrival when everyone said the mechanic there was excellent. Our breakdown occurred on a Saturday, so we had to wait until Monday before anyone could look at the boat. When the repair was complete, we received an unexpected surprise. As we were paying our repair bill, the owner said there would be no slip rental fee, as we were waiting for the repairs to be completed. Next morning we left early in order to arrive at the Cape Fear River with the tide and were treated to a beautiful sunrise.

After leaving Masonboro we passed through Snow's Cut to the Cape Fear River. As we proceeded south we kept greens cans on our right. These, however, are marked for the waterway and have yellow triangles on them advising ICW travelers to keep them on the right.

The Cape Fear River has a number of range markers to help you stay in the channel, and we found them very helpful. Once they were lined up, we knew we were in the middle.

Photo 90

Range marks on Cape Fear River. The front mark must line up with the back mark, if you are to remain in the channel.

Cruising South – What To Expect Along The ICW – *Joan Healy*

Photo 91

A ferry crosses Cape Fear River.

At this point we decided that if we were going to spend money to stay in a marina, we should plan ahead to take advantage of all it offered. When you arrive at a marina late in the day, there's little time to do anything except have dinner and sleep. We really wanted to see the towns, so we checked the waterway guide for a marina with an anchorage within five or ten miles. Then we could anchor for the night and reach the marina in the morning.

There's always some work to do when you are at a marina. The boat needs washing to remove the salt spray and clothes also have to be laundered. I'd do some baking while we were plugged into shore power. These tasks only took a short time. The remainder of the day we visited nearby towns to learn all we could about the area.

Proceeding south, we passed a sign on a dock that read, "Smile. Your wake is being recorded." We found most boaters on the ICW to be very courteous and conscious of the fact that a boater is responsible for his wake. Many captains would call on the radio and ask us to slow down so they could pass us with little or no wake. There were even a few who asked on which side we wanted them to pass. We always appreciated this, especially in a narrow channel.

Photo 92

Everywhere you look there is another NO-WAKE sign.

Photo 93

Sunset Beach pontoon bridge. It's fascinating to watch.

Chapter Eight
South Carolina and Georgia

Soon after crossing the state line, we knew we were in South Carolina. There were three golf courses along the banks in the first 20 minutes. We passed under a cable car ferrying golfers from one side of the waterway to the other.

Photo 94

Cable car ferrying golfers.

A great deal of new home construction was under way in South Carolina on both sides of the Waterway. New bridges were being built to accommodate these new residents.

Photo 95

A new high-level bridge being built in South Carolina.

We planned to spend our first night in South Carolina at Barefoot Landing, an outlet mall, which was listed in our anchorage guide. It provides a wall for boaters to tie up overnight at no charge. We enjoyed a pleasant walk, wandering in and out of shops and watching fish in the ponds before heading back to the boat for the night.

Photo 96

Swing bridge at Barefoot Landing.

As we motored the next morning we noticed the engine was losing speed and power, and RPM's kept falling We anchored just out of the channel and replaced the water separator filter which corrected the problem.

Photo 97

Socastee RR bridge is normally open.

Because of the time spent replacing the filter, it was late in the afternoon as we headed toward Georgetown. It became almost impossible to read numbers on the buoys or differentiate the square from the triangle because we were looking directly into the sun.

Photo 98

Nests make markers hard to distinguish.

We finally found the markers and turned into the Sampit River. The waterway guide advised the starboard channel would take us into Georgetown. We also heeded the advice to stay well clear of the starboard shoreline because of old pilings.

In addition to the dinghy dock, the ambience of Georgetown makes boaters feel welcome. As we stepped off the dock we were in the middle of town with all conveniences within walking distance. The Visitor's Center is located on the waterfront and we were able to get maps of South Carolina and Georgetown.

Photo 99

The anchorage at Georgetown is very popular.

Photo 100

Industry at Georgetown, S.C.

Cruising South – What To Expect Along The ICW – *Joan Healy*

Leaving the anchorage, we headed out the river and into the ICW in Winyah Bay. For a distance the ICW follows the markers on Winyah Bay, which lead to the ocean, so we kept the green cans on our right. After checking the chart, I knew which was the last green marker to follow before looking for red nuns on our right that lead into a narrow channel. We had gone only a short distance when we saw flashing yellow lights ahead which was a sign for a ferry crossing.

Traveling through this part of South Carolina, we passed national forests and wildlife refuges. The banks were covered with trees and grasses. The ICW meandered back and forth, and we made numerous turns as it followed the paths of streams and rivers. At times it seemed as if boats were sailing toward us through the grass. There are times when it doesn't seem to make sense to follow the markers. I had to remind myself that the buoys were taking us where there is enough water. Even as I questioned the path, we always followed them. Your eyes play tricks on you, especially when you are looking out over a long distance and the sun is shining bright. We trusted our charts and followed the buoys.

Weather forecasts in this part of the country list the high and low tides along with temperature and winds. Tides were something we were still getting used to. We'd see tree roots completely exposed during low tide and wonder how those trees survived. Trees where we live would die if their roots were exposed to direct sunlight.

We were learning about tide, but not fast enough. Our guide listed Whiteside Creek as a good anchorage with plenty of water so we decided to spend the night there. A few other boats passed the creek, but did not come in to anchor. It was our private anchorage.

After dinner we decided to watch a video. Halfway through the movie I tried to get up and couldn't. We were heeled over. Because we had both been sitting down, we hadn't noticed when the boat began to heel. The stern of the boat was very close to shore, so trying to kedge off would be impossible because our rudder sat in the mud. We had checked the depth when we anchored but hadn't compensated for the fact that the tide would be going out. As the water rushed out the creek, our boat swung with the force of the current, pushing the stern over to the shallow bank and we now sat at an angle. We decided all we could do was set the alarm clock for high tide and hope the returning tide would lift us.

We checked the tide tables, set the alarm, went to bed, slept very uncomfortably on an angle and got up at 2 a.m. When the tide reversed, the water poured in the creek. We were again impressed with the force of water. This little creek that had appeared absolutely calm as we sat and enjoyed the view in the evening now had a strong current in it. The water level rose, we were again floating, and our rudder was out of the mud. We shortened the rode to keep the boat in the middle and went back to bed until 0600 when we left for Charleston.

Photo 101

Regulations posted at Ben Sawyer Bridge north of Charleston.

As we entered Charleston harbor, the task was determining which buoys to follow. The buoys from the inlet led ocean going ships out of the harbor. Two rivers, the Ashley and the Cooper, also come into the harbor, which is very large.

Charleston is magnificent. Ashley Marina, where we stayed, had a van to chauffeur boaters into the town where we walked through the historic district. Once again walking proved to be the best way to see the homes and, especially, the gardens. Most of the homes had wrought iron gates in front which we peeked through to view the magnificent gardens. Every square inch of space was incorporated in the landscaping, all very formal. Many homes had nameplates with dates from the 1700's and some stated the home had belonged to signers of the Declaration of Independence.

Photo 102

Wapoo Creek bridge sign showing channel to call and clearance overhead.

After leaving Charleston we anchored in Church Creek. From there the Waterway took us into the North Edisto River, which was filled with dolphin. The banks in this area are lovely copper tones, and the greens of the grasses complement the banks.

Beaufort S.C. gave us our first close-up view of old live oaks. The branches of these trees reach down towards the ground. We passed streets with clearance signs posted to warn high vehicles of tree branches hanging low over the street.

The next morning at 0700 we left Factory Creek, Beaufort, passed through Lady's Island swing bridge and entered the Beaufort River. A short distance from Beaufort, we entered the Port Royal Sound.

Photo 103

Fishing boat on Port Royal Sound.

Heading south past Paris Island and Hilton Head we remembered the warnings about water depth in this area. We were trying to be vigilant to avoid shallow water. On the approach to the Savannah River, we again had to determine where mid-channel was, with markers on only one side. We'd slowed down because our depth meter kept indicating there was not a lot of water under our boat. Ahead we spotted a green marker, the first one in a long while. With the green buoy in sight, we tried to bring the boat to, what appeared to be, mid-channel before turning into the Savannah River. We did this without consulting the chart to determine if this was an ICW buoy. In fact, the green marker in the distance was a Savannah River buoy. As we steered to what we thought was the center of the channel, we hit bottom. I take blame for this, because if I had prudently checked our chart, I would have known. The worst part was that the tide was going down. We knew we would sit here for a while, so we had lunch and waited. As other boats approached, some called on the radio and asked if we were aground or anchored. Others just called, and we told them all to stay to the right. For a while we were a navigational aid. More than one captain said, "I went aground there last year."

After a few hours, the water slowly came back in but not enough to float us. We spotted a large freighter coming up the river and got ready to start our engine as the freighter passed. Its wake gave us just enough lift, and we were free This time we stayed close to the red buoys and entered the Savannah River for the short trip across. We lost valuable hours waiting for the tide to rise. As a consequence, we knew we wouldn't have enough daylight left to reach a marina.

This illustrates an important point: fill your water tanks at every opportunity, even if your plan calls for being somewhere water is available. There will be days when you anticipate arriving at a marina but circumstances can change your plans. I kept track of how often we had to refill our tanks and found we could go between four and five days on average. I marked the log each time so I would have an approximate idea of when we needed to refill.

St. Augustine Creek was nearby. This time after we dropped anchor, Paul took the dinghy out to check the depth all around in case the boat would swing during the night. Again, we were alone but could see other masts in the distance.

Next morning we headed out, anticipating a visit to Savannah. We found the Isle of Hope Marina and after docking, it was only about a three-block walk to a bus stop. We asked the bus driver to let us off at the best place to see the city, whereupon he took us to the Welcome Center. We once again were impressed with southern hospitality.

The highlight of Savannah was the River Walk. In this

area, old cotton warehouses were refurbished and now contain shops and restaurants. Where walls are exposed, you can see they're are two feet thick.

After leaving the marina we were detained at the Skidaway Narrows bridge, as the bridge operator was waiting for an ambulance to cross. While waiting we were joined by nine other sailboats, so when the bridge finally opened we all sailed through, looking like a flotilla.

Photo 104

Skidaway Narrows Bridge.

Just past St. Simon's Island we decided to depart from the ICW and go up the Brunswick River to visit Brunswick, Ga. The trip was short and the river was well marked.

Cruising South – What To Expect Along The ICW – Joan Healy

Photo 105

Bridge under construction to replace Sidney Lanier Bridge on Brunswick River.

After leaving Brunswick we followed the buoys in the river that lead to Jekyll Creek. A danger sign warned to stay in the channel because of a submerged jetty at the entrance to the creek. Even in the channel we noted there was not much water under our boat.

At Jekyll Island we experienced the first marina with a swimming pool and hot tub. We enjoyed both. The marina had bikes to loan, so we took advantage of them to tour the island. We rode past stately homes that were referred to as "cottages" and had belonged to tycoons who at one time owned the whole island.

We were almost to Florida. As we crossed Cumberland Sound which separates Georgia from Florida, Paul, looking ahead, said with disbelief in his voice, "That looks like a submarine coming towards us." A few moments later a Coast Guard boat pulled alongside and a crewman told us we'd have to get out of the channel until the submarine passed.

Photo 106

Sub and tender at dock in Cumberland Sound.

Photo 107

Sub and tugs.

Photo 108

One of those times when sailboats yield the right of way.

Chapter Nine
Welcome to Florida

We passed Fort Clinch on the tip of Amelia Island as we turned into the Amelia River.

Photo 109

Fort Clinch at the tip of Amelia Island.

Our first stop was Fernandina Beach on Amelia Island. Fernandina Harbor Marina has a long outer wall for transient dockage, but we chose to anchor and use the dinghy dock. On our first trip ashore we were surprised to see power boats docked in the slips behind the outer wall, sitting in mud and sailboats over on their side. The tide here is about four feet and when we came ashore, the tide was out.

Cruising South – What To Expect Along The ICW – *Joan Healy*

Photo 110

Fernandina Harbor at low tide.

We decided the boaters in this area had to be very cognizant of the daily tide fluctuations in order to use their boats at all.

One of the attractions was the Palace Saloon, which claims to be the oldest bar in Florida. (Tobacco Road in Miami in fact holds State Liquor License #1.) It looks today much the same as it did when millionaires from Cumberland Island would come over and rub elbows with the shrimpers. The carved oak bar is 40 feet long with caryatids supporting the entablature. In days gone by, bartenders would encourage patrons to toss coins into the dishes that the caryatids held. Our bartender told us not many coins settled in the dishes, but the bartenders collected a good supply off the floor when the bar closed.

After remaining five days, we left Fernandina at high tide and wondered what this stretch of the Waterway was like at low tide. We next stopped at Fort George River, an excellent anchorage. As we entered, we favored the starboard side as the anchorage guide had cautioned. Once anchored we took our dinghy to shore to visit the Kingsley Plantation on Fort George Island operated by the National Park Service. It's worth your visit as well.

The ICW crosses the St. Johns River between Jacksonville and Mayport. If you turn to go up the St. Johns river you will come into Jacksonville. We turned. Our timing was poorly planned, and much of the day was a struggle against a strong current but our very slow pace gave us a chance to see both sides of the river and all the activity.

Jacksonville is a very busy port, and as we neared, we encountered four bridges within a mile of each other. Each is a different color.

Photo 111

One of Jacksonville's many bridges.

Just past the center of Jacksonville we entered the Trout River and docked for a short time. From here we took the dinghy to the Jacksonville Zoo, which incredibly has a dinghy dock. Much of the zoo is a natural setting, making it seem as if the animals roam free and the spectators are fenced off.

From the Trout River we went back into the St. John's to the Ortega River on the outskirts of Jacksonville. We planned to stay at the Ortega River Boat Yard for a few days to check on having our boat shipped back home in March.

Photo 112

View from marina on the Ortega River, with Florida's most-opened bridge in the background.

The marina was in walking distance of a large mall, a good grocery store and two marine stores where we were able to restock the boat.

The morning we intended to leave Jacksonville, a heavy fog set in. We couldn't see the other side of the river. When it lifted, we still had time to make the bridge and go downstream with the current until we experienced a delay at the bridge. There was a mechanical problem and the operator was waiting for it to be repaired. Despite the wait, our trip back to the ICW was easier than the trip up.

Photo 113

Palm Valley Bridge.

St. Augustine was the next city we planned to visit. The waterway guide advised extreme caution. As we neared the inlet the buoys appeared to take us way out of our way and lead us towards the inlet. We had been warned not to cut the corner, to follow all of the buoys and be sure we went around #60 on the ocean side. As Paul steered, I was the lookout to insure we saw and followed all the small green buoys that lead to #60. We saw another sailboat that had not heeded the warning, resting on her side just before the inlet. It had become a navigational aid, just as we had been, as we sat on our side at the entrance to the Savannah River.

Our arrival was timed perfectly. We arrived on the first weekend of December, when St. Augustine officially starts its Nights of Lights festival. We dropped anchor near the Bridge of Lions and could see the Castillo de San Marcos, the old Spanish fort. In fact, while we were at anchor here, we jumped more than once as the cannon was fired at Castillo de San Marcos.

Photo 114

Lights on the Bridge of Lions.

Photo 115

The green light is on when the bridge is open.

The Spanish influence is seen in the cathedral, the fort, college, homes and the street names. Visitors crowded the streets as town merchants and residents prepared for the Illumination of the City. Our nation's oldest city truly knows how to welcome visitors. The city sparkled with tiny white lights, 1,250,000 in all, on buildings, trees, bushes, and the Bridge of Lions. Just outside a gallery door in an open courtyard, a guitar player serenaded us.

Cruising South – What To Expect Along The ICW – Joan Healy

Photo 116

Anchored boats at St Augustine, with city in background.

Photo 117

Boat anchored in front of Castillo de San Marcos at St. Augustine.

Leaving St. Augustine, scenery along the waterway changes. We no longer experienced whole days of seeing nothing. Now one side of the ICW remained in the natural state, and on the opposite shore, homes crowded the banks. In some areas both sides were built up. Still, it was still possible to find places to anchor.

Photo 118

Anchorage in front of cement plant.

Later in the day while passing Daytona, we saw a new high fixed bridge under construction and wondered if it will replace one of the three lift bridges.

Photo 119

Bridge construction at Daytona.

New Smyrna Beach was another town that provided a wall for boaters. Next to the wall is a pleasant town park with swings similar to those in Beaufort, SC where one can sit and watch boats on the waterway. From the park it was only a short walk to the grocery store.

We left the wall and anchored a short distance down the waterway and watched dolphin all around us.

Mosquito Lagoon is a favorite spot for manatees. Manatees are very slow swimmers, and cannot move away from fast boats so many are injured each year by propellers.

Photo 120

Manatee zone with restrictions listed.

Photo 121

Manatee zone, with ICW exemption.

Mosquito Lagoon is a large body of water, but only the dredged channel is navigable. At the end of Mosquito Lagoon you enter Haulover Canal which leads to the Indian River Lagoon. As you enter the canal, you can see Cape Canaveral in the distance. Stay in the channel. The shallow water outside the channel attracts scores of dolphin, white pelicans and cormorants and we enjoyed the show as we cruised slowly past them.

Photo 122

White pelicans were a treat to behold.

Indian River Lagoon is dotted with numerous small islands called spoil islands. These were made from material dredged from the river channels.

A short distance before Titusville we passed a bascule railroad bridge that is normally open. A note on the chart tells boaters that it will close automatically if a train is approaching and lights on the bridge will signal boaters. When flashing green lights turn to flashing red, a siren will give four blasts. This siren repeats and after an eight minute delay, the bridge closes.

Photo 123

Jay Jay railroad bridge in the open position.

Our next stop was Cocoa Beach. As at every new town, we located a tourist guidebook that stated a jazz concert was presented in the Gazebo every Friday at lunch time, all year round. Being a jazz fan, I decided to attend the concert while Paul did some maintenance. I was one of the first to arrive, and as I watched the other spectators come in, realized everyone knew each other. They came with folding chairs and box lunches. One woman approached me when she noticed my T-shirt from our National Public Radio station in Buffalo and inquired if I was reporter. I said "No", but I don't think she believed me. The president of the jazz society brought me an ice cream cone. I guess they were either extremely friendly or they all thought I was a reporter and wanted to insure a favorable review.

After leaving Cocoa, we meandered down the waterway to the large dragon on the tip of Merritt Island. Dragon Point is the intersection of the Banana and Indian River Lagoon and is a favorite anchorage of many cruisers.

Photo 124

Dragon Point is a popular anchorage.

The farther south we traveled in Florida, the more crowded the Waterway and the surrounding land became. Marine traffic became heavier, the number of bridges increased, and the distance between bridges decreased.

Photo 126

Jupiter Lighthouse.

Cruising South – What To Expect Along The ICW – *Joan Healy*

Photo 127

Boats pass several bridges near Jupiter.

We were planning to go home for the holidays but had reserved a slip for one month to get a better rate. We'd been doing a lot of anchoring and thought some nights in a marina would be welcome.

Living at a marina is easy to get used to. Many of the conveniences you do without on a boat are available. The days spent there before and after our trip home were very relaxing. We took dinghy rides up the Waterway and into smaller areas nearby. We were close enough that we could walk to the ocean for a swim.

Our time was starting to get short now, so we had to decide where we would spend our last two months.

In West Palm Beach many boats were anchored near the Blue Heron Causeway and Peanut Island. This anchorage is popular because it's next to the Lake Worth Inlet. We dropped anchor and as we watched to make sure it was set, we noticed the boats in this anchorage were not all facing the same way. In most anchorages as the wind and current shift, all boats will turn the same way. Here, boats faced various directions.

Some boaters were using this as a stopover before leaving for the Bahamas, others were live aboards who had jobs in the area.

One day a new boat came in as we were taking our dinghy ashore. On one side of the rudder it said Ber and on the other, lin. As I tried to say it, I realized it was Berlin. We talked to them on our way back out to the boat and found out they were from Germany.

This anchorage satisfied all our needs: beaches, swimming and shopping, all easily available. We could go out on the ocean every day we wished to sail and, more important, could pick the perfect weather conditions. In addition, we had made arrangements to have our boat shipped home from a marina just across the Waterway. We decided to spend the balance of our cruise in this anchorage.

Chapter Ten
Getting Ready to Go Home

It didn't seem possible, but it was time to start preparing the boat to be shipped home. All the arrangements had been made in January and, back then, March seemed far away.

Photo 128

Preparing for the trip home.

The sails had to be removed, folded and bagged. Anchors were taken off and stowed. The bimini, dodger, sea kettle and life rings were all brought inside. The inside of the boat was filling up fast. We made sure all perishable food was gone. Anything breakable was wrapped. Everything that was to remain had to be secured. We took one last look around our anchorage and started across the ICW to the marina where our boat would be put on a truck. All the water had to be drained and antifreeze added for the trip to cold weather.

Photo 129

Meantime *hauled out in Florida.*

Photo 130

Meantime *going to the blocks in Buffalo.*

Cruising South – What To Expect Along The ICW – Joan Healy

As we packed and stowed, we thought about what we had learned and all we could look forward to in the future. It still amazes me we did this, a dream for so many years. We were sad as we prepared to go home but knew there would be many more trips.

There's always more to learn, and always another place to go.

Cruising South – What To Expect Along The ICW – *Joan Healy*

Appendix One
Suppliers & Manufacturers

The following list of Suppliers and Manufacturers does not constitute a complete directory of all the fine manufacturers and suppliers available throughout the country. This in no way indicates you should only deal with these companies; as always ask your friends for their recommendations. In most cases you will not be disappointed following their guidance.

AFI: Teak accessories, shelving and organizers. 2655 Napa Valley Corporate Dr., Napa, CA 94558
Alaska Diesel Electric: Engines, 206-789-3880, 4420 14 Ave. N.W., Seattle, WA 98107-0543
Balmar: Alternators and Controls, 902 N.W. Ballard Way, Seattle, WA 98107
Boat/US: Boat Supplies, 800-937-2628, 880 S Pickett St. Alexandria, VA 22304
Camping World, RV Furnishings & Accessories, 800-893-1923, Three Springs Rd., Bowling Green, KY 42102
Caterpillar: Engines, 800-447-4986, 2001 Ruppman Plaza, Peoria, IL 61614
Cummings Marine: Engines, 803-745-1171, 4500 Leeds Ave., Suite 301, Charleston, SC 29405
Datamarine International, Inc.: Electronics Instruments, 508-

563-7151, 53 Portside Drive, Pocasset, MA 02559
Davis Instruments: Navigation Instruments and Marine Accessories, 415-732-9229, 3465 Diablo Ave., Hayward, CA 94545
Daytona Marine Engine Corp.: Engines, 904-676-1140, 1815 N. U. S. 1, Ormond Beach, FL 32174
Defender: Boat Supplies, 800-628-8225, P O Box 820 New Rochelle, NY 10802-0820
Depco Pump Co: Pump supplies and parts, 813-446-1656, 1227 S Linoln Ave., Clearwater, FL 34616
Detroit Diesel: Engines, 313-592-5000, 13400 Outer Drive W., Detroit, MI 48239
Deutz MWM/KHD Canada: Engines, 514-335-3150, 4420 Garand, Ville St. Laurent, Quebec, Canada H4R 2A3
Diesel Engineering & Marine Services: Engine repair and parts, 800-742-1169, P O Box 276, Port Salerno, FL 34992
Dometic: Galley Equipment, 219-294-2511, fax 912-293-9686, P O Box 490, Elkhart, IN 46515
E & B Discount Marine: Boat Supplies, 800-262-8464, P O Box 3138, Edison, NJ 08818-3138
Espar Heater Systems: Cabin Heaters, 416-670-0960, 6435 Kestrel Road, Mississauga, Ontario, Canada L5T 128
Fastening Solutions, Inc.: Heavy-Duty Grips, 800-232-7836, fax 818-997-1371, E-mail fastening@earthlink.net, Web site www.Fasteningsolutions.com, 15230 Burbank Blvd., Suite 106, Van Nuys, CA 91411
Fireboy Halon Systems Division-Convenience Marine Products, Inc.: Fire Suppression Equipment, 616-454-8337, P O Box 152, Grand Rapids, MI 49501
Furuno USA Inc.: Electronics, 415-873-4421, P O Box 2343, South San Fransico, CA 94083
Galley Maid Marine Products, Inc.: Galley, Water Supply and Waste, 407-848-8696, 4348 Westroads Drive, West Palm Beach, FL 33407
General Electric Company, Appliance Park, Louisville, KY 40225

Cruising South – What To Expect Along The ICW – Joan Healy

Get Organized: Storage Space Products, 800-803-9400, 600 Cedar Hollow Rd., Paoli, PA 19301, Web site www.getorginc.com
Gougeon Brothers, Inc.: West System Epoxy, 517-684-7286, PO Box 908, Bay City, MI 48707
Hammacher Schlemmer & Company: Unusual Products, 212 W. Superior, Chicago, IL 60610
Heart Interface Corp.: Inverters, Chargers, Monitors, Electrical, 1-800-446-6180, 21440 68th Ave. S., Kent, WA 98032
Home Depot: Tools/Supplies, Located in most cities throughout the country. Look in local phone book.
Hubbell Wiring Device Division, Hubbell Inc.: Electrical products, 203-337-3348, P O Box 3999, Bridgeport, CT 06605
Icom America, Inc.: Electronics, 206-454-8155, 2380 116th Ave. NE, Bellevue, WA 98004
InterCon Marketing Inc., Lighting and Boat Accessories, 1121 Lewis Ave., Sarasota, FL 34237. Web site www.interconmktg.com. E-mail icmmktg@gte.net
Interlux Paints: Varnish, Paint, Coatings, 908-964-2285, 2270 Morris Ave, Union, NJ 07083
Jamestown Distributors: Boat Building/Repairing Supplies, 800-423-0030, 28 Narragansett Ave., P O Box 348, Jamestown, RI 02835
Jenn-Air Company: Cooktop and Ranges, 3035 Shadeland, Indianapolis IN 46226
Lehman's Hardware and Appliances, Box 41, Kidron OH 44636 supplies the Amish, who do not use electricity. It's an excellent source of everything from treadle sewing machines and gas refrigerators to hand-cranked radios and washing machines. www.lehmans.com or e-mail info@lehmans.com. Tel. 330-857-5757 to order a catalog, which costs $4.
Lister-Petter, Ltd: Engines, 913-764-3512, 815 E. 56 Highway, Olathe, KS 66061
Magellan's, 110 W. Sola St., Santa Barbara, CA 93101, 800-

Cruising South – What To Expect Along The ICW – Joan Healy

962-4943 or www.magellans.com sells travel products including electrical adapters for any system worldwide, security wallets, and a kit containing sterile syringes and sutures.

MAN Marine Engines: Engines, 954-771-9092, 6555 NW 9th Ave., Suite 306, Ft. Lauderdale, FL 33309

Marinco Electrical Products: Electrical products, 415-883-3347, One Digital Drive, Novato, CA 94949

Marine Propulsion: Genset & Transmission Repair, 561-283-6486, 3201 S. E. Railroad Ave., Stuart, FL 34997

Marine Corporation Of America: Engines, 317-738-9408, 980 Hurricane Road, Franklin, IN 46131

Mattresses in custom sizes, shapes and fillings are available from Handcraft Mattress Company, 531 E. Goetz, Santa Ana CA 92707. A sleep system that can be tailored to individual comfort, with dual controls, is available from Americana, 888-565-7211 or www.rvaccessories.com. Custom airbeds are available from 800-508-1008.

MerCruiser: Engines, 405-743-6704, Stillwater, OK 74075

Micrologic: Electronics, 818-998-1216, 20801 Dearborn Street, Chatsworth, CA 91311

New England Ropes, Inc.: All types of line, 508-999-2351, Popes Island, New Bedford, MA 02740

Nitro-Pak Preparedness Center, 475 W. 910 S. Be Prepared Way, Heber, UT 84032, 800-866-4876, www.nitro-pak.com. Fax orders to 888-648-7672. Primarily a supply house for Mormons and others to whom preparedness is a way of life, this company is also a good source of water filters in all types and sizes, multi-fuel lamps, freeze-dried foods and MREs, first aid and dental kits, and other items for the adventurous liveaboard.

Onan: Gensets, 612-574-5000, 1400 73rd Ave. N.E., Minneapolis, MN 55432

Origo, InterCon Marketing Inc.: Stoves and Refrigeration Kits, 1121 Lewis Ave., Sarasota, FL 34237

Paneltronics: Electrical Panels, 305-823-9777, 11960 NW 80th Ct, Hialeah Gardens, FL 33016

PCD, Professional Cutlery Direct, offers cutlery, cookware and chef's tools for the serious galley cook. Everything is professional quality. Request a catalog, PCD, 242 Branford Road, North Branford, CT 06471, 800-859-6994 or www.cutlery.com

Poly-Planar Inc.: Waterproof Marine Speakers, Box 2578, Warminster, PA 18974. Webiste www.polyplanar.com

Powerline: Alternators and Controls, 1-800-443-9394, 4616 Fairlane Ave, Ft Worth, TX 76119

R&R Textiles: Custom Deck Mats, 800-678-5920, 503-786-3678, 5096 Hwy. 76, Chatsworth, GA 30705. Web site www.rrrtextiles.com

Racor Division-Parker Hannifin Corporation: Fuel Filters, 800-344-3286, P O Box 3208, Modesto, CA 95353

Raritan Engineering Company, Inc.: Heads, Treatment Systems, Charging Systems, 609-825-4900

Ray Jefferson Company: Electronics, 215-487-2800, Main & Cotton Sts., Philadelphia, PA 19127

Raytheon Marine Company: Electronics, 603-881-5200, 46 River Road, Hudson, NH 03051

Resolution Mapping: Electronic Charts and Software, 617-860-0430, 35 Hartwell Ave., Lexington, MA 02173

Sea Recovery Corporation: Water Purification, 213-327-4000, P O Box 2560, Gardena, CA 90247

Seagull Water Purification Systems: Water Purification, 203-384-9335, P O Box 271, Trumbull, CT 06611

SeaLand Technology: Marine Heads, 800-321-9886 or 330-496-3211, Fax 330-496-3097, P. O. Box 38, Big Prairie, OH 44611

Star Brite: Coatings/Sealants, 305-587-6280, 4041 S W 47th Ave., Ft. Lauderdale, FL 33314

Statpower Technologies Corp: Chargers, Inverters, 7725 Lougheed Hwy, Burnby, BC, Canada V5A 4V8

Teak Deck Systems: Teak Deck Caulking, 813-377-4100, 6050 Palmer Blvd., Sarasota, FL 34232

The Guest Company, Inc.: Electrical Components, Chargers, Inverters, 203-238-0550, P O Box 2059, Station A, Meriden, CT 06450

Trace Engineering: Chargers, Inverters, 206-435-8826, 5917 195th N.E., Arlington, WA 98223

U-Line Corporation: Ice Maker and Refrigeration, 414-354-3000, fax 414-354-7905, Web site www.u-line.com, E-mail u-line@execpc.com, P O Box 23220, Milwaukee, WI 53223

Unlimited Quality Products: Noise Reduction, 602-462-5235, 800-528-8291, 710 W. Broadway Rd #508, Mesa, AZ 85210

Upholstery Journal/Marine Textiles: Magazine, P O Box 14268, St. Paul, MN 55114

Vanner Weldon Inc.: Inverters & Chargers, 614-771-2718, 4282 Reynolds Dr., Hilliard, OH 43026-1297

Vermont Country Store: Table Cloths, P O Box 3000, Manchester Ctr., VT 05255

Webasto Heater, Inc.: Cabin Heaters, 313-545-8770, 1458 East Lincoln, Madison Hts., MI 48071

West Marine: Boat Supplies, 800-538-0775, P O Box 50050, Watsonville, CA 95077-5050

Westerbeke: Engines, 617-588-7700, Avon Industrial Park, Avon, MA 02322

Woolsey/Z-Spar: Paint, Varnish, Coatings, 800-221-4466, 36 Pine St, Rockaway, NJ 07866

Yanmar Diesel America Corp.: Engines, 708-541-1900, 901 Corporate Drive, Buffalo Grove, IL 60089-4508

Appendix Two
Tools & Supplies

This list has been compiled through the joint effort of our staff and many contributing writers.

As you delve deeper into boating, you will always find a need for one more tool, or a few more supplies. It is truly a case of "Too much is never enough and enough is always too much." With this in mind it is best to adapt the following to your boat's needs and storage capacity.

The boat tools should not be shared with the car or the home. Purchase a good quality plastic tool box larger than the current need. Remove the handle which will certainly come off when you are transferring the box to the boat or the dock. A second box for less used tools is also a good idea.

* Tools for a small cruising sailboat without electrical or plumbing systems.

** Tools to add to the list for a mid-sized cruiser with electrical, plumbing, electronics and an inboard engine.

*** Tools for the long-term cruiser or liveaboard sailor intending to make most of the repairs to most of the systems.

The balance of the list will be needed at your land base for extensive repairs, renovations, upgrades and restoration projects.

HAND TOOLS

Good brands will carry a life time warranty.
* # 1, #2, #3 Phillips screwdrivers.
* Thin blade 3/16", medium blade 1/4", heavy blade 3/8" straight screwdrivers.

All the above should also be purchased in the stubby length.
** Jewelers set of screwdrivers.
** Various square drivers if you have this type of fastener on your boat. You will have to know the sizes you will need.
* Linesman pliers.
** Dikes/side cutters.
** Wire strippers. Buy the type with the stripper portion before the hinge.
** Terminal crimps.
** Digital multi-meter.
* Long-nose pliers.
** Needle-nose pliers.
* Vise Grips
* Small slip joint pliers (opens to 2").
*** Straight blade sheet metal cutters.
** Caulk gun.
*** Lufkin folding rule with brass slide extension.
** Large and small metal files.
* Set of allen wrenches 1/16" to 7/16" minimum.
*** China bristles paint brushes with an angle cut, in sizes 1", 1-1/2", 2", 2-1/2".
** School pencils.
** Pencil sharpener.
** Thin blade awl.
* 8" & 12" adjustable wrench.
** 12" Lenox hacksaw with 18, 24, & 32 teeth per inch blades.
** Estwing leather handle straight claw hammer.
*** A #2, & #3 nail set.
** Combination wrench set.
** 1/4" drive socket set.

* 3/8" drive socket set.
** Ignition wrench set.
The term "set" is used because most of these tools are sold in sets. You can purchase them individually but you will spend more than buying a set.
** 24" to 36" adjustable wrench. The size will depend on the prop nut size of your boat.
** Battery carrying strap.
** Feeler gauges (blade type).
** Cordless drill with two batteries, charger, cobalt drill bits ranging from 1/32" to 3/8" and screwdriver bits with a good holder. These should be the same size as your hand screwdrivers.
** Large slip joint pliers (opens to 4").
*** 2# Ballpeen hammer.
Caulking iron.
*** Rubber mallet.
*** Small & large Wonder bars.
*** Diston small dovetail saw.
*** Diston coping saw.
*** Diston 13 point hand saw.
*** Stanley 25' tape measure.
*** Stanley combination square.
*** Stanley #40 wood chisels 1/2", 3/4", 1".
*** Block plane.
*** Half round wood file/rasp.
*** Heavy blade awl.
*** Larger size drill bits 7/16" to 1" forsener bits are the best for large wood bits. Metal bits should be cobalt.
*** Brad point bits 1/16" to 3/8".
Plug cutters 3/8" to 3/4"
*** Hole saw set.
*** Metal chisel and drift set.
** Right angle-straight and Phillips screwdrivers.
** Fish tape.
** Heavy gauge terminal crimp tool.
** Line wrench set.

Cruising South – What To Expect Along The ICW – Joan Healy

** 1/2" drive socket set.
** Deep well socket set for all the different size drives you now own. Some of these may have been included when you purchased the sets.
*** 1/2" Breaker bar.
*** 1/2" Click stop torque wrench.
** 1/2" drive large sockets for all the bolts/nuts which are larger than the sets contain.
** Wrenches for the same bolts/nuts.

POWER TOOLS

Purchase brand name, heavy duty, commercial grade tools with a high ampere draw. These are the only tools that will last.
3/8" & 1/2" power drills.
Circular saw with good carbide tooth blades.
*** Random orbiting sander with 5" & 6" pads. Buy your 3M gold sanding disk in the 6" size and cut them down when you need the 5" size. Buy rolls of these grits. 60, 80, 100, 120, 150, 180.
Power miter box with an 80 tooth carbide blade.
3" x 24" or 4" x 24" belt sander. Buy at least three belts of each of these grits. 36, 80, 100, 120.
*** Soldering gun with electrical solder and flux.
Heat gun.
*** Random orbit buffer if you own a fiberglass boat.
Scrolling jigsaw with various wood and metal blades.
Router with various bits purchased as the jobs warrant. Always use roller bearing bits where applicable.
*** Sawz-all with various size and types of blades for wood/metal.
Biscuit jointer with at least two hundred of the two larger size biscuits.
*** 25', 50', & 75' #12 wire extension cords.
Table or radial arm saw. The radial arm saw can be set up with

a multitude of attachments to handle many different functions other than cross cutting and ripping.

SUPPLIES
All Stainless Steel Fasteners

** At least 50 each of these Phillips head screws.
#4 x 1/2", 3/4", 1" Flat and oval head.
#6 x 1/2", 3/4", 1", 1-1/4", 1-1/2", 1-3/4", 2" Flat and oval head.
#8, #10, #12 Same as #6 plus 2-1/2", 3" Flat and oval head.
** Finish washers for each of the above size screw numbers.
#6, #8, #10, 1/2", 3/4", 1", 1-1/2" Pan head.
** At least 10 each of these fasteners.
1/4" x 20 x 2", 3", 4" Flat and stove head bolts with 2 washers and 1 nut each.
5/16" & 3/8" x 1", 1-1/2", 2", 2-1/2", 3" machine bolts with 2 washers and 1 nut each.
** Cap nuts for each of the above sizes.
*** 1/4" x 2", 3", 4", 5" lag bolts with washers.
** Large fender washers for each of the above sizes.
*** 2 pieces of solid rod 3' long in 1/4", 3/8", 1/2".
*** 2 pieces of threaded rod 3' long with 6 nuts and washers per piece in 1/4", 3/8", 1/2".
* Various size cotter pins to replace ones which will need to be removed. Check the sizes you need before ordering or purchase a cotter pin kit with various sizes included.
18 gauge brass or stainless steel brads in 1/2", 3/4", 1"

ELECTRICAL

** Butt terminals, male and female quick disconnect terminals. Order at least 50 each for wire gauges, 22-18, 16-14, 12-10, 8.
** Spade connectors, stud connectors. Order at least 50 each for the same gauge of wire above to fit around stud

sizes 4-6, 8-10, 1/4", 5/16", 3/8".
*** 10 terminals for each size battery cable in use on your boat.
** 6 battery clamps (lugs, the kind used on your car) with stud. Do not connect the battery wires directly to the clamp; use the stud and terminals.
** 200 each of 6" & 11" medium duty wire ties.
*** 100 each of 3/4" and 1-1/2" cable clamps.
*** 1 each 4, 6, 8, 10 position terminal blocks. 6 each 20 amp in-line fuse holders with 5 each of, 5 amp, 10 amp, 15 amp, & 20 amp fuses.
*** 100 ft each of wire gauges 18, 16, 14, 12, 10, 8. Tinned marine primary wire.
*** 25 ft each of wire gauges 6 & 4.
*** 10 butt connectors for 6 & 4 wire.
*** 10 ft of battery cable for each size you have in use on board.
*** 2 ft each of heat shrink tubing 3/16", 1/4", 3/8", 1/2," 3/4".

MISC. ELECTRICAL SUPPLIES

** Liquid electrical tape.
** Vinyl electrical tape.
** Nylon string to use as a wire fishing device.
** 1 Pair of battery jumper cables. They must be long enough to reach between the banks of batteries you may need to jump. If you can not find them this long, make up your own with heavy ends and # 2 battery cable.
** Jumper wires for testing. These can be made with 4 alligator clips and 12 gauge wire.
** 1 breaker or fuse holder for each different size and type you on have board.
** 1 fuse for each specialty fuse on board.
** 1 switch for each type on board.
** 2 extra bulbs for each type on board.
** 1 lamp socket for each type on board.

*** 1 of each shore line end or an extra 50' shore line set.
** 1 connector for each type of electronic instrument connector on board.

SEALANTS, PAINT AND REPAIR PRODUCTS

** 1 tube each of Teak Deck Systems, 3M 5200 in white, GE silicone in white & clear, Star Bright polysulfide underwater sealant, Sea Repair.
** 1 small kit each of Epoxy, Marine Tex, Boat Yard fiberglass with 6 oz. cloth and matching gel coat colors.
*** 1 qt each of varnish, top sides paint for each color on board, stain, paint thinner, acetone, lacquer thinner, Penatrol, boiled linseed oil.
*** Coffee cans.
*** Plastic pots in 1 qt size.
*** Disposable brushes in 1/2", 1", 1-1/2", 2", 2-1/2".

PLUMBING PARTS

* The best method of determining your needs for plumbing will be to go through your supply and waste systems measuring each hose, clamp, tubing and fitting type and size. With this list in hand purchase at least two of each type of fitting, 10 of each size clamp, hose to replace the longest length of each size or fittings and hose to patch in the very long lengths. As with your shore power line, carry an extra water supply hose of no less than 50'. Also purchase water hose repair ends.

** This may not be considered plumbing by some, but it carries water, therefore it is included in this section. Your engines have many small sizes and lengths of hoses. As with the plumbing hoses, buy enough to replace the longest length of each size with the proper size clamps. These should be the heavy wall hose with wire reinforcement.

** If you have large exhaust lines you do not need to carry a full length. Do carry a large coffee can with 4 hose clamps which are a larger size than the exhaust hose. You must carry at least one spare impeller or a rebuilding kit with the impeller included for every pump on board. THIS IS A MUST!

MISC. SUPPLIES

* Shock cords and ends.
* Buckets.
* Sponges.
* Chamois.
** Toilet brush.
** Scrub brush.
** Deck brush with handle.
*** Roller handle, pan and pads.
** Bronze wool.
** Bronze scrub brush.
** Detergents.
** Cleaning products.
** Polishes.
** Compounds.
** Water resistant/proof glue.
*** Extension cord ends.
** Patching material for every inflatable on board.
** Repair parts for engine(s).
*** Antifreeze.
** Oils.
** Grease gun with grease.
** Transmission fluid.
* 5 gals of extra fuel.
* Duct tape.
* Riggers tape.
*** Masking tape.
*** Sheet sand paper in grits 50, 80, 100, 120, 150, 180, 220.

At least 5 sheets of each grit.
* At least two complete sets of dock lines and anchor rodes.
* One 3/4" line (regardless of boat size to 45') three times the length of the boat. (Tow line)

Cruising South – What To Expect Along The ICW – Joan Healy

Appendix Three
Glossary

This glossary has been compiled through a joint effort of the staff of Bristol Fashion Publications and many authors. It is not intended to cover the many thousands of words and terms in the language exclusive to boating. The longer you are around boats and boaters, the more of this language you will learn.

A

Accumulator tank - A tank used to add air pressure to the freshwater system thus reducing water pump run time.
Aft - Near the stern.
Amidships - Midway between the bow and the stern.
Antifouling - Bottom paint used to prevent growth on the boat bottom.
Athwartships - Any line running at a right angle to the fore/aft centerline.

B

Backer plate- Metal plate used to increase the strength of a through bolt application, such as with the installation of a cleat.
Ballast - Weight added to improve a boat's sea handling abilities of the boat or to counterbalance an unevenly loaded boat.

Beam - The widest point of the boat.
Bilge - The lowest point inside a boat.
Bilge pump - Underwater water pump used to remove water from the bilge.
Binnacle - A box or stand used to hold the compass.
Bolt - Any fastener with any head style and machine thread shank.
Boot stripe - Contrasting trim paint of a contrasting color located just above the bottom paint on the hull sides.
Breaker - Replaces a fuse to interrupt power on an electrical circuit when that circuit becomes overloaded or shorted.
Bridge - The steering station of a boat.
Brightwork - Polished metal or varnished wood aboard a boat.
Bristol Fashion - The highest standard of condition any vessel can obtain and the highest state of crew seamanship. The publishing company that brought you this book.
Bulkhead - A wall running across (athwartships) the boat.
Butt connectors - A type of crimp connector used to join two wires end to end in a continuing run of the wire.

C

Canvas - A general term used to describe cloth used for boat coverings. A type of cloth material.
Carlin - A structural beam joining the inboard ends of deck beams that are cut short around a mast or hatch.
Cavitation - Reduced propeller efficiency due to vapor pockets in areas of low pressure on the blades. Turbulence caused by prop rotation that reduces the efficiency of the prop.
Centerboard - A hinged board or plate at the bottom of a sailboat of shallow draft. It reduces leeway under sail.
Chafing gear - Any material used to prevent the abrasion of another material.
Chain - Equally sized inter-looping oblong rings commonly used for anchor rode.

Chain locker - A forward area of the vessel used for chain storage.

Chine - The intersection of the hull side with the hull bottom, usually in a moderate-speed to fast hull. Sailboats and displacement-speed powerboats usually have a round bilge and do not have a chine. Also, the turn of the hull below the waterline on each side of the boat. A sailboat hull, displacement hull and semi-displacement hull have a round chine. Planing hulls all have a hard (sharp corner) chine.

Chock - A metal fitting used in mooring or rigging to control the turn of the lines.

Cleat - A device used to secure a line aboard a vessel or on a dock.

Clevis - A Y-shaped piece of sailboat hardware about two to four inches long that connects a wire rope rigging terminal to one end of a turnbuckle.

Coaming - A barrier around the cockpit of a vessel to prevent water from washing into the cockpit.

Cockpit - Usually refers to the steering area of a sailboat or the fishing area of a sport-fishing boat. The sole of this area is always lower than the deck.

Companionway - An entrance into a boat or a stairway from one level of a boat's interior to another.

Cribbing - Large blocks of wood used to support the boat's hull during it's time on land.

Cutlass Bearing® - A rubber tube that is sized to a propeller shaft and fits inside the propeller shaft strut.

D

Davit - Generally used to describe a lifting device for a dinghy.

Delaminate - A term used to describe two or more layers of any adhered material that have separated from each other because of moisture or air pockets in the laminate.

Device - A term used in conjunction with electrical systems.

Generally used to describe lights, switches receptacles, etc.

Dinghy - Small boat used as a tender to the mother ship.

Displacement - The amount of water, in weight, displaced by the boat when floating.

Displacement Hull - A hull that has a wave crest at bow and stern and settles in the wave trough in the middle. A boat supported by its own ability to float while underway.

Dock - Any land based structure used for mooring a boat.

Draft - The distance from the waterline to the keel bottom. The amount of space (water) a boat needs between its waterline and the bottom of the body of water. When a boat's draft is greater than the water depth, you are aground.

Dry rot - This is not a true term as the decay of wood actually occurs in moist conditions.

F

Fairing - The process of smoothing a portion of the boat so it will present a very even and smooth surface after the finish is applied.

Fairing compound - The material used to achieve the fairing process.

Fairlead - A portion of rigging used to turn a line, cable or chain to increase the radius of the turn and thereby reduce friction.

Fall - The portion of a block and tackle system that moves up or down.

Fastening - Generally used to describe a means by which the planking is attached to the boat structure. Also used to describe screws, rivets, bolts, nails etc. (fastener)

Fiberglass - Clothlike material made from glass fibers and used with resin and hardener to increase the resin strength.

Filter - Any device used to filter impurities from any liquid or air.

Fin keel - A keel design that often resembles an up-side-down "T" when viewed from fore or aft.

Flame arrestor - A safety device placed on top of a gasoline carburetor to stop the flame flash of a backfiring engine.

Flat head - A screw head style that can be made flush with or recessed into the wood surface.

Float switch - An electrical switch commonly used to automatically control the on-off of a bilge pump. When this device is used, the pump is considered to be an automatic bilge pump.

Flying bridge - A steering station high above the deck level of the boat.

Fore - The front of a boat.

Fore-and-aft - A line running parallel to the keel. The keel runs fore-and-aft.

Forecastle - The area below decks in the forwardmost section. (pronunciation is often fo'c's'le)

Foredeck - The front deck.

Forward - Any position in front of amidships.

Freeboard - The distance on the hull from the waterline to the deck level.

Full keel - A keel design with heavy lead ballast and deep draft. This keel runs from the bow, to the stern at the rudder.

G

Galley - Kitchen.

Gelcoat - A hard, shiny coat over a fiberglass laminate that keeps water from the structural laminate.

Gimbals - A method of supporting anything that must remain level regardless of the boat's attitude.

Grommet - A ring pressed into a piece of cloth through which a line can be run.

Gross tonnage - The total interior space of a boat.

Ground tackle - Refers to the anchor, chain, line and connections as one unit.

H

Hanging locker - A closet with a rod for hanging clothes.
Hatch - An opening with a lid that open in an upward direction.
Hauling - Removing the boat from the water. The act of pulling on a line or rode is also called hauling.
Hawsehole - A hull opening for mooring lines or anchor rodes.
Hawsepipes - A pipe through the hull, for mooring or anchor rodes.
Head - Toilet. Also refers to the entire area of the bathroom.
Helm - The steering station and steering gear.
Holding tank - Used to hold waste for disposal ashore.
Hose - Any flexible tube capable of carrying a liquid.
Hull - The structure of a vessel not including any component other than the shell.
Hull lines - The drawing of the hull shape in plan, profile and sections (body plan).

I

Inboard - Positioned toward the center of the boat. An engine mounted inside the boat.

K

Keel - A downward protrusion running fore and aft on the center line of any boat's bottom. It is the main structural member.
King plank - The plank on the center line of a wooden laid deck.
Knees - A structural member reinforcing and connecting two other structural members. Also, two or more vertical beams at the bow of a tugboat used to push barges.

L

Launch - To put a boat into the water.
Lazarette - A storage compartment in the stern of a boat.
Lead - The material used for ballast.
Limber holes - Holes in the bilge timbers to allow water to run to the lowest part of the bilge, where it can be pumped out.
LOA - Length Over All. The over all length of a boat.
Locker - A storage area.
Log - A tube or cylinder through which a shaft or rudder stock runs from the inside to the outside. The log will have a packing gland (stuffing box) on the inside of the boat. Speed log is used to measure distance traveled. A book used to a keep record of the events on board a boat.
LWL - Length on the Waterline. The length of a boat at the water line.

M

Manifold - A group of valves connected by piping to tanks to allow filling and removal from one or more tanks.
Marine gear - Boat's transmission.
Mast - An upward pointing timber used as the sail's main support. Also used on power and sailboats to mount flags, antennas and lights.
Mile - A statute mile (land mile) is 5280 feet. A nautical mile (water mile) or knot is 6080.2 feet.
Mizzen mast - The aftermost mast on a sailboat.

N

Nautical mile - A distance of 6080.2 feet
Navigation lights - Lights required to be in operation while underway at night. The lighting pattern varies with the type, size and use of the vessel.
Nut - A threaded six-sided device used in conjunction with a bolt.

Nylon - A material used for lines when some give is desirable. Hard nylon is used for plumbing and rigging fittings.

O

Oval head - A screw head used when the head can only be partially recessed. The raised (oval) portion of the head will remain above the surface.
Overhangs - The length from the bow or stern ending of the waterline to the forward or aft end of the hull.

P

Painter - A line used to tow or secure a small boat or dinghy.
Pan head - A screw head with a flat surface, used when the head will remain completely above the surface.
Panel - A term used to describe the main electrical distribution point, usually containing the breakers or fuses.
Pier - Same general use as a dock.
Pile - A concrete or wooden post driven or otherwise embedded into the water's bottom.
Piling - A multiple structure of piles.
Pipe - A rigid, thick-walled tube.
Planing hull - A hull design, which under sufficient speed, will rise above it's dead-in-the-water position and seem to ride on the water.
Planking - The covering members of a wooden structure.
Plug - A type of pipe, tubing or hose fitting. Describes any device used to stop water from entering the boat through the hull. A cylindrical piece of wood placed in a screw hole to hide the head of the screw.
Port - A land area for landing a boat. The left side when facing forward.
Propeller (Prop, Wheel, Screw) - Located at the end of the shaft. The prop must have at least two blades and propels the vessel through the water with a screwing motion.

R

Radar - A electronic instrument which can be used to "see" objects as blips on a display screen.

Rail - A nonstructural safety member on deck used as a banister to help prevent falling overboard.

Reduction gear - The gear inside the transmission housing that reduces the engine rpm to a propeller shaft Rpm that is optimum for that hull and engine.

Ribs - Another term for frames. The planking is fastened to these structural members.

Rigging - Generally refers to any item placed on the boat after the delivery of the vessel from the manufacturer. Also refers to all the wire rope, line, blocks, falls and other hardware needed for sail control.

Ring terminals - A crimp connector with a ring that can have a screw placed inside the ring for a secure connection.

Rode - Anchor line or chain.

Rope - A term that refers to cordage and this term is only used only on land. When any piece of cordage is on board a boat, it is referred to as line or one of it's more designating descriptions.

Round head - A screw or bolt head with a round surface that remains completely above the material being fastened.

Rudder - Located directly behind the prop and used to control the steering.

Rudder stock - Also known as rudder post. A piece of round, solid metal attached to the rudder at one end and the steering quadrant at the other.

S

Samson post - A large piece of material extending from the keel upward through the deck and used to secure lines for mooring or anchoring.

Screw - A threaded fastener. A term for propeller.

Screw thread - A loosely spaced, coarse thread used for wood and sheet metal screws.

Sea cock - A valve used to control the flow of water from the sea to the device it is supplying.

Shackle - A metal link with a pin to close the opening. Commonly used to secure the anchor to the rode.

Shaft - A solid metal cylinder that runs from the marine gear to the prop. The prop is mounted on the end of the shaft.

Shear pin - A small metal pin that inserted through the shaft and propeller on small boats. If the prop hits a hard object, the pin will "shear" without causing severe damage to the shaft.

Sheaves - The rolling wheel in a pulley.

Sheet metal screw - Any fastener that has a fully threaded shank of wood screw threads.

Ship - Any seagoing vessel. To ship an item on a boat means to bring it aboard.

Shock cord - An elastic line used to dampen the shock stress of a load.

Slip - A docking space for a boat. A berth.

Sole - The cabin and cockpit floor.

Spade rudder - A rudder that is not supported at its bottom.

Stability - The ability of a hull to return to level trim after being heeled by the forces of wind or water.

Stanchion - A metal post that holds the lifelines or railing along the deck's edge.

Starboard - The right side when facing forward.

Statute mile - A land mile. 5280 feet.

Stem - The forwardmost structural member of the hull.

Step - The base of the mast where the mast is let into the keel or mounted on the keel in a plate assembly.

Stern - The back .

Strut - A metal supporting device for the shaft.

Stuffing box - The interior end of the log where packing is inserted to prevent water intrusion from the shaft or rudder stock.

Surveyor - A person who inspects the boat for integrity and

safety.

Switch - Any device, except breakers, that interrupts the flow of electrical current to a device.

T

Tachometer - A instrument used to count the revolutions of anything turning, usually the engine, marine gear or shaft.

Tack rag - A rag with a sticky surface used to remove dust before applying a finish to any surface.

Tank - Any large container that holds a liquid.

Tapered plug - A wooden dowel tapered to a blunt point and is inserted into a seacock or hole in the hull in an emergency.

Tender - A small boat (dinghy) used to travel between shore and the mother ship. A boat with limited stability is said to be tender.

Terminal lugs - Car-style, battery cable ends.

Through hull (Thru hull) - Any fitting between the sea and the boat that goes "through" the hull material.

Tinned wire - Stranded copper wire with a tin additive to prevent corrosion.

Topsides - Refers to being on deck. The part above the waterline.

Torque (or Torsion) - The rotating force on a shaft. (lb-in)

Transmission - Refers to a marine or reduction gear.

Transom - The flat part of the stern.

Trim - The attitude with which the vessel floats or moves through the water.

Trip line - A small line made fast to the anchor crown. When weighing anchor this line is pulled to back the anchor out and thus release the anchor's hold in the bottom.

Tubing - A thin-walled metal or plastic cylinder, similar to pipe but having thinner walls.

Turn of the bilge - A term used to refer to the corner of the hull where the vertical hull sides meet the horizontal hull bottom.

Turnbuckles - In England, they are called bottle screws. They secure the wire rope rigging to the hull and are used to adjust the tension in the wire rope.

V

Valves - Any device that controls the flow of a liquid.

Vessel - A boat or ship.

VHF radio - The electronic radio used for short-range (10 to 20 mile maximum) communications between shore and vessels and between vessels.

W

Wake - The movement of water as a result of a vessel's movement through the water.

Washer - A flat, round piece of metal with a hole in the center. A washer is used to increase the holding power of a bolt and nut by distributing the stress over a larger area.

Waste pump - Any device used to pump waste.

Waterline - The line created at the intersection of the vessel's hull and the water's surface. A horizontal plane through a hull that defines the shape on the hull lines. The actual waterline or just waterline, is the height at that the boat floats. If weight is added to the boat, it floats at a deeper waterline.

Water pump - Any device used to pump water.

Wheel - Another term for prop or the steering wheel.

Whipping - Any method used, except a knot, to prevent a line end from unraveling.

Winch - A device used to pull in or let out line or rode. It is used to decrease the physical exertion needed to do the same task by hand.

Windlass - A type of winch used strictly with anchor rode.

Woodscrew - A fastener with only two-thirds of the shank

threaded with a screw thread.

Y

Yacht - A term used to describe a pleasure boat, generally over twenty-five feet. Usually used to impress someone.

Yard - A place where boats are stored and repaired.

Z

Zebra mussel - A small, freshwater mussel that will clog anything in a short period of time.

Cruising South – What To Expect Along The ICW – Joan Healy

Current Books Published by
Bristol Fashion Publications
Free catalog, phone 1-800-478-7147

Boat Repair Made Easy — Haul Out
Written By John P. Kaufman

Boat Repair Made Easy — Finishes
Written By John P. Kaufman

Boat Repair Made Easy — Systems
Written By John P. Kaufman

Boat Repair Made Easy — Engines
Written By John P. Kaufman

Standard Ship's Log
Designed By John P. Kaufman

Large Ship's Log
Designed By John P. Kaufman

Custom Ship's Log
Designed By John P. Kaufman

Designing Power & Sail
Written By Arthur Edmunds

Building A Fiberglass Boat
Written By Arthur Edmunds

Buying A Great Boat
Written By Arthur Edmunds

Boater's Book of Nautical Terms
Written By David S. Yetman

Practical Seamanship
Written By David S. Yetman

Captain Jack's Basic Navigation
Written By Jack I. Davis

Creating Comfort Afloat
Written By Janet Groene

Living Aboard
Written By Janet Groene

Racing The Ice To Cape Horn
Written By Frank Guernsey & Cy Zoerner

Marine Weather Forecasting
Written By J. Frank Brumbaugh

Complete Guide To Gasoline Marine Engines
Written By John Fleming

Complete Guide To Outboard Engines
Written By John Fleming

Complete Guide To Diesel Marine Engines
Written By John Fleming

Trouble Shooting Gasoline Marine Engines
Written By John Fleming

Skipper's Handbook
Written By Robert S. Grossman

White Squall - The Last Voyage Of Albatross
Written By Richard E. Langford

Cruising South
What to Expect Along The ICW
Written By Joan Healy

Electronics Aboard
Written By Stephen Fishman

Five Against The Sea
A True Story of Courage & Survival
Written By Ron Arias

Scuttlebutt
Seafaring History & Lore
Written By Captain John Guest USCG Ret.

Cruising The South Pacific
Written By Douglas Austin

Catch of The Day
How To Catch, Clean & Cook It
Written By Carla Johnson

VHF Marine radio Handbook
Written By Mike Whitehead

Electric Propulsion For Boats
Written By Charles Mathys

Cruising South – What To Expect Along The ICW – Joan Healy

About The Author

Joan Healy didn't come from a long line of boaters. No one in her immediate family owned a boat, so her boating experience was minimal and confined to invitations from friends. It wasn't until her youngest child was in high school that she and her husband purchased a canoe and a true love affair began.

When she and her husband purchased a sailboat, there was more to learn. Joan took classes in sailing, and as her knowledge grew, so did her enjoyment. Soon she was teaching both seamanship, piloting and enjoying every spare moment aboard.

This is her first nautical book, and with it she hopes to share some of the knowledge she has gained during her years of cruising the ICW from the Erie Barge Canal to Palm Beach, Florida.

www.ingramcontent.com/pod-product-compliance
Lightning Source LLC
Chambersburg PA
CBHW020357170426
43200CB00005B/207